interchange

FIFTH EDITION

T0306683

3

Workbook

Jack C. Richards

with Jonathan Hull and Susan Proctor

CAMBRIDGE
UNIVERSITY PRESS

CAMBRIDGE
UNIVERSITY PRESS & ASSESSMENT

Shaftesbury Road, Cambridge CB2 8EA, United Kingdom

One Liberty Plaza, 20th Floor, New York, NY 10006, USA

477 Williamstown Road, Port Melbourne, VIC 3207, Australia

314–321, 3rd Floor, Plot 3, Splendor Forum, Jasola District Centre, New Delhi – 110025, India

103 Penang Road, #05–06/07, Visioncrest Commercial, Singapore 238467

Torre de los Parques, Colonia Tlacoquemécatl del Valle, Mexico City CP 03200, Mexico

Cambridge University Press & Assessment is a department of the University of Cambridge.

We share the University's mission to contribute to society through the pursuit of education, learning and research at the highest international levels of excellence.

www.cambridge.org
Information on this title: www.cambridge.org/9781316622766

First published 1991
Second edition 1998
Third edition 2005
Fourth edition 2013
Fifth edition 2017
Fifth edition update published 2021

20 19 18

Printed in Great Britain by CPI Group (UK) Ltd, Croydon CR0 4YY

A catalogue record for this publication is available from the British Library

ISBN 978-1-009-04052-5 Student's Book 3 with eBook
ISBN 978-1-009-04053-2 Student's Book 3A with eBook
ISBN 978-1-009-04054-9 Student's Book 3B with eBook
ISBN 978-1-009-04075-4 Student's Book 3 with Digital Pack
ISBN 978-1-009-04077-8 Student's Book 3A with Digital Pack
ISBN 978-1-009-04078-5 Student's Book 3B with Digital Pack
ISBN 978-1-316-62276-6 Workbook 3
ISBN 978-1-316-62277-3 Workbook 3A
ISBN 978-1-316-62279-7 Workbook 3B
ISBN 978-1-108-40711-3 Teacher's Edition 3
ISBN 978-1-316-62230-8 Class Audio 3
ISBN 978-1-009-04079-2 Full Contact 3 with Digital Pack
ISBN 978-1-009-04080-8 Full Contact 3A with Digital Pack
ISBN 978-1-009-04081-5 Full Contact 3B with Digital Pack
ISBN 978-1-108-40307-8 Presentation Plus 3

Additional resources for this publication at cambridgeone.org

Contents

Credits

The authors and publishers acknowledge the following sources of copyright material and are grateful for the permissions granted. While every effort has been made, it has not always been possible to identify the sources of all the material used, or to trace all copyright holders. If any omissions are brought to our notice, we will be happy to include the appropriate acknowledgements on reprinting and in the next update to the digital edition, as applicable.

Key: BL = Below Left, BR = Below Right, C = Centre, CL = Centre Left, CR = Centre Right, TC = Top Centre, TL = Top Left, TR = Top Right.

Illustrations

337 Jon (KJA Artists): 51; **Mark Duffin**: 31, 80; **Pablo Gallego** (Beehive Illustration): 10, 20; **Thomas Girard** (Good Illustration): 4, 28, 53; **Dusan Lakicevic** (Beehive Illustration): 1, 14, 22, 33, 96; **Yishan Li** (Advocate Art): 6, 13, 65; **Quino Marin** (The Organisation): 29; **Gavin Reece** (New Division): 3, 64; **Paul Williams** (Sylvie Poggio Artists): 15, 66.

Photos

Back cover (woman with whiteboard): Jenny Acheson/Stockbyte/GettyImages; Back cover (whiteboard): Nemida/GettyImages; Back cover (man using phone): Betsie Van Der Meer/Taxi/GettyImages; Back cover (woman smiling): PeopleImages.com/DigitalVision/GettyImages; Back cover (name tag): Tetra Images/GettyImages; Back cover (handshake): David Lees/Taxi/GettyImages; p. 2 : Michael H/DigitalVision/GettyImages; p. 5 (TL): Jade/Blend Images/Getty Images Plus/GettyImages; p. 5 (TR): Jamie Grill/GettyImages; p. 5 (BL): Blend Images - Jose Luis Pelaez Inc/Brand X Pictures/GettyImages; p. 5 (BR): Tomasz Trojanowski/Hemera/Getty Images Plus/GettyImages; p. 7: John Rowley/Photodisc/GettyImages; p. 8: KidStock/Blend Images/GettyImages; p. 9: monkeybusinessimages/iStock/Getty Images Plus/GettyImages; p. 12 (TL): ColorBlind/The Image Bank/GettyImages; p. 12 (TR): Sigrid Gombert/MITO images/GettyImages; p. 12 (CL): 4x6/E+/GettyImages; p. 12 (CR): Roy Hsu/Photographer's Choice RF/GettyImages; p. 13 (TR): mediaphotos/iStock/Getty Images Plus/GettyImages; p. 16: Purestock/GettyImages; p. 17 : PeopleImages/DigitalVision/GettyImages; p. 18: Phil Boorman/Cultura/GettyImages; p. 19 (TL): Robert George Young/Photographer's Choice/GettyImages; p. 19 (BR): dangdumrong/iStock/Getty Images Plus/GettyImages; p. 21 (TR): Chris Dyball/Innerlight/The Image Bank/GettyImages; p. 21 (CL): MattStansfield/iStock/Getty Images Plus/GettyImages; p. 23: EXTREME-PHOTOGRAPHER/E+/GettyImages; p. 24 (Johnson): George Doyle/Stockbyte/GettyImages; p. 24 (Marshall): Digital Vision./Photodisc/GettyImages; p. 24 (James): Yellow Dog Productions/The Image Bank/GettyImages; p. 24 (Grant): wdstock/iStock/Getty Images Plus/GettyImages; p. 24 (Simpson): Dave and Les Jacobs/Blend Images/GettyImages; p. 25 (TR): asiseeit/iStock/Getty Images Plus/GettyImages; p. 25 (BR): hadynyah/E+/GettyImages; p. 26: Thomas_EyeDesign/Vetta/GettyImages; p. 30: Education Images/Universal Images Group/GettyImages; p. 32 (George): snapphoto/E+/GettyImages; p. 32 (airport): Philippe TURPIN/Photononstop/Photolibrary/GettyImages; p. 32 (Diane): Vesnaandjic/E+/GettyImages; p. 32 (car): lisegagne/E+/GettyImages; p. 34: Whiteway/E+/GettyImages; p. 35 (wrench): TokenPhoto/E+/GettyImages; p. 35 (TR): John E. Kelly/Photodisc/GettyImages; p. 36: pixelfusion3d/iStock/Getty Images Plus/GettyImages; p. 37 (drain): belovodchenko/iStock/Getty Images Plus/GettyImages; p. 37 (plane): incposterco/E+/GettyImages; p. 37 (smoke): Harrison Shull/Aurora/GettyImages; p. 37 (land): Sierralara/RooM/GettyImages; p. 38 (forest): Ro-Ma Stock Photography/Photolibrary/GettyImages; p. 39: Howard Shooter/Dorling Kindersley/GettyImages; p. 40: VCG/Contributor/Visual China Group/GettyImages; p. 41: Travel Ink/Gallo Images/The Image Bank/GettyImages; p. 42: SolStock/iStock/Getty Images Plus/GettyImages; p. 43: Doug Armand/Oxford Scientific/GettyImages; p. 44: Wilfried Krecichwost/DigitalVision/GettyImages; p. 45: cglade/E+/GettyImages; p. 46 (TL): Lew Robertson/StockFood Creative/GettyImages; p. 46 (TC): Alina555/iStock/Getty Images Plus/GettyImages; p. 46 (TR): Jose Luis Pelaez Inc/Blend Images/GettyImages; p. 47 (photo 1): Hemera Technologies/PhotoObjects.net/Getty Images Plus/GettyImages; p. 47 (photo 2): Picturenet/Blend Images/GettyImages; p. 47 (photo 3): Zoran Milich/Photodisc/GettyImages; p.47 (photo 4): DragonImages/iStock/Getty Images Plus/GettyImages; p. 48 (TR): BrianAJackson/iStock/Getty Images Plus/GettyImages; p. 48 (CR): reka prod./Westend61/GettyImages; p. 49 (TR): simazoran/iStock/Getty Images Plus/Getty Image; p. 49 (CR): ONOKY - Eric Audras/Brand X Pictures/GettyImages; p. 49 (BR): michaeljung/iStock/Getty Images Plus/GettyImages; p. 50: leaf/iStock/Getty Images Plus/GettyImages; p. 52 (TL): IP Galanternik D.U./E+/GettyImages; p. 52 (TR): Lady-Photo/iStock/Getty Images Plus/GettyImages; p. 54: Westend61/GettyImages; p. 55 (CR): Andy Sheppard/Redferns/GettyImages; p. 55 (BR): by Roberto Peradotto/Moment/GettyImages; p. 56 (L): Mint/Hindustan Times/GettyImages; p. 56 (R): Michael Runkel/imageBROKER/GettyImages; p. 57: Bettmann/GettyImages; p. 58 (TL): Bettmann/GettyImages; p. 58 (BR): Ron Levine/Photographer's Choice/GettyImages; p. 59: Windsor & Wiehahn/Stone/GettyImages; p. 60: Javier Pierini/Stone/GettyImages; p. 61: blackred/iStock/Getty Images Plus/GettyImages; p. 62: izusek/iStock/Getty Images Plus/GettyImages; p. 63: ADRIAN DENNIS/AFP/GettyImages; p. 67: Greg Vaughn/Perspectives/GettyImages; p. 68: Caiaimage/Robert Daly/GettyImages; p. 69 (TL): marco wong/Moment/GettyImages; p. 69 (TR): Oscar Wong/Moment Open/GettyImages; p. 69 (CL): Otto Stadler/Photographer's Choice/GettyImages; p. 69 (CR): David Hannah/Lonely Planet Images/GettyImages; p. 69 (BL): LOOK Photography/UpperCut Images/GettyImages; p. 69 (BR): lightkey/E+/GettyImages; p. 70: Thomas Kokta/Photographer's Choice RF/GettyImages; p. 71 (Calgary Farmers' Market): Ken Woo/Calgary Farmers' Market; p. 71 (WWF): © naturepl.com/Andy Rouse/WWF; p. 72: Christian Hoehn/Taxi/GettyImages; p. 73 (TL): Rosanna U/Image Source/GettyImages; p. 73 (TC): Mark Weiss/Photodisc/GettyImages; p. 73 (TR): i love images/Cultura/GettyImages; p. 73 (BL): monkeybusinessimages/iStock/Getty Images Plus/GettyImages; p. 73 (BC): Photo and Co/The Image Bank/GettyImages; p. 73 (BR): Alija/E+/GettyImages; p. 74 (stonehenge): Maxine Bolton/EyeEm/GettyImages; p. 74 (people): Peter Dennis/GettyImages; p. 74 (boats): De Agostini/M. Seemuller/De Agostini Picture Library/GettyImages; p. 75 (bigfoot): Big_Ryan/DigitalVision Vectors/GettyImages; p. 75 (footprints): Danita Delimont/Gallo Images/GettyImages; p. 76: Steve Bronstein/Stone/GettyImages; p. 77: kbeis/DigitalVision Vectors/GettyImages; p. 78: mediaphotos/Vetta/GettyImages; p. 79 (T): Oscar Garces/CON/LatinContent Editorial/GettyImages; p. 81: Theo Wargo/Getty Images North America/GettyImages; p. 82 (TL): ColorBlind Images/Blend Images/GettyImages; p. 82 (TR): track5/E+/GettyImages; p. 83: imagenavi/GettyImages; p. 84 (TL): John Wildgoose/Caiaimage/GettyImages; p. 84 (TR): Bloomberg/GettyImages; p. 84 (CL): Chris Ryan/Caiaimage/GettyImages; p. 84 (CR): numbeos/E+/GettyImages; p. 84 (BL): Tom Merton/OJO Images/GettyImages; p. 84 (BR): Ariel Skelley/Blend Images/GettyImages; p. 85 (TL): marcoventuriniautieri/E+/GettyImages; p. 85 (TR): Anadolu Agency/GettyImages; p. 85 (CL): Caspar Benson/GettyImages; p. 85 (CR): Jake Olson Studios Blair Nebraska/Moment/GettyImages; p. 86 (house): Peter Baker/GettyImages; p. 86 (traffic): Levi Bianco/Moment/GettyImages; p. 86 (bike): Billy Hustace/The Image Bank/GettyImages; p. 86 (using mobile): SolStock/E+/GettyImages; p. 87: Image Source/DigitalVision/GettyImages; p. 89: Caiaimage/Paul Bradbury/Riser/GettyImages; p. 90: Dawid Garwol/EyeEm/GettyImages; p. 92: FatCamera/E+/GettyImages; p. 93: c.Zeitgeist/Everett/REX/Shutterstock; p. 94 (TR): shapecharge/E+/GettyImages; p. 94 (BR): borgogniels/iStock/Getty Images Plus/GettyImages; p. 95: Lucidio Studio, Inc./Moment/GettyImages.

1 That's my kind of friend!

1 Complete these descriptions with the words from the list.

1. Eric is so ___modest___! He always has such great ideas and never takes any credit for them.
2. The Wongs like meeting new people and having friends over for dinner. They're one of the most ____________ couples I know.
3. You can't trust Alice. She always promises to do something, but then she never does it. She's pretty ____________.
4. James wants to be an actor. It's hard to break into the business, but his family is very ____________ of his dream.
5. I never know how to act around Lisa! One minute she's in a good mood, and the next minute she's in a bad mood. She's so ____________.

- [x] modest
- [ ] outgoing
- [ ] supportive
- [ ] temperamental
- [ ] unreliable

2 Opposites

A Complete the chart by forming the opposites of the adjectives in the list. Use *in-* and *un-*. Then check your answers in a dictionary.

- [x] attractive
- [ ] reasonable
- [ ] helpful
- [ ] flexible
- [ ] dependent
- [x] competent
- [ ] reliable
- [ ] popular
- [ ] formal
- [ ] experienced
- [ ] cooperative
- [ ] sensitive

Opposites with *in-*		Opposites with *un-*	
incompetent	____________	unattractive	____________
____________	____________	____________	____________
____________	____________	____________	____________

B Write four more sentences using any of the words in part A.

1. Alan is very incompetent at work. He makes a lot of mistakes.
2. ______________________________
3. ______________________________
4. ______________________________
5. ______________________________

3 Add *who* or *that* to the conversation where necessary. Put an ✗ where *who* or *that* is not necessary.

A: I'm looking for someone ___✗___ I can go on vacation with.

B: Hmm. So what kind of person are you looking for?

A: I want to travel with someone ________ is easygoing and independent.

B: Right. And you'd probably also like a person ________ is reliable.

A: Yeah, and I want someone ________ I know well.

B: So why don't you ask me?

A: You? I know you too well!

B: Ha! Does that mean you think I'm someone ________ is high-strung, dependent, and unreliable?

A: No! I'm just kidding. You're definitely someone ________ I could go on vacation with. So, . . . what are you doing in June?

4 Complete the sentences with *who* or *that* and your own information or ideas.

1. I generally like to go out with people _who are easygoing and have a sense of humor_.
2. I'd rather travel with someone ________________.
3. I don't really want a roommate ________________.
4. My classmates and I like teachers ________________.
5. My best friend and I want to meet people ________________.
6. Most workers would prefer a boss ________________.
7. Some people don't like stingy types ________________.
8. I don't want to have inflexible friends ________________.
9. I feel comfortable discussing my problems with friends ________________.
10. My favorite friends are people ________________.

5 Two of a kind?

A Read the article. What six personality types are discussed?

DO OPPOSITES ATTRACT EACH OTHER?

Some psychologists believe that we are attracted to people who seem to have the characteristics that we wish we had. For example, if you love music but don't play an instrument, you might be attracted to someone who is a musician. Being with that person allows you to be close to something that is important to you and that you want more of in your life.

Because people are very complex, we can be attracted to several different kinds of people who are our opposites in one way or another. So let's take a look at six principal kinds of characteristics in people, and you can decide which type you are most like and which type is your opposite.

Let's begin with introverted and extroverted people. Introverted people often spend a lot of time inside their minds and can be quiet and reserved. Extroverted people enjoy getting out and spending time with other people. If opposites attract, then there will always be an interest between introverted and extroverted people. Introverted people will get out of their minds and into the world with their extroverted friends or partners, while extroverted people will appreciate the quiet space of the inner world of their introverted friends or partners.

Then there are people who relate to the world from a thinking perspective and others who relate to it from a feeling perspective. Thinkers can be cool and objective in their judgments, while feelers may be warm and passionate about theirs. Because people who spend a lot of time thinking want to feel deeply too, they may be attracted to a feeling kind of person. And someone who is very aware of their own powerful feelings may enjoy the company of a relaxed and logical thinker.

Two other characteristics are those of people who use their five senses to understand the world we live in as opposed to those who use their intuition. Sensing people are very aware of the present moment; they are realistic and practical people. Intuitive people, on the other hand, often spend their time in a future of infinite possibilities where their imagination is as free as a bird. The attraction here could be that intuitive people realize they need the practical know-how of sensing people in order to make their dreams come true. Likewise, the sensors are attracted to the imaginative possibilities they see in intuitive people.

These three different pairs of personality characteristics – the introvert and the extrovert, the thinker and the feeler, and the sensor and the intuitive – are of course found in each individual person. Yet many psychologists believe that a person will more often use one characteristic of each pair, in the same way that people use either their left hand or their right. And, according to the idea that opposites attract, the left hand needs the right hand in the same way that the right hand needs the left!

B Based on the information in the article, what kind of people are you attracted to? Circle the words. Then, using the idea that opposites attract, complete the next sentence with the type of person *you* must be.

1. I am more attracted to a person who is (introverted / extroverted). Therefore, I am ____________.
2. I am more attracted to a person who is a (thinker / feeler). Therefore, I am a ____________.
3. I am more attracted to a person who is the (sensing type / intuitive type). Therefore, I am a ____________.

C Do you agree with the kind of person you seem to be according to part B? Why or why not?

____

6 Match the clauses in column A with the most suitable clauses in column B.

A	B
1. I like it _____	**a.** when someone criticizes me in front of other people.
2. I don't mind it _____	**b.** when people are easygoing and friendly.
3. It upsets me _____	**c.** when rich people are stingy.
4. It embarrasses me _____	**d.** when people are a few minutes late for an appointment.

7 Write sentences about these situations. Use the expressions in the box.

I love it . . .	**I can't stand it . . .**	**I don't like it . . .**
It upsets me . . .	**It bothers me . . .**	**I don't mind it . . .**
I really like it . . .	**It makes me happy . . .**	**It makes me angry . . .**

1. *I don't like it when people cut in line.*

2. ______________________________

3. ______________________________

4. ______________________________

5. ______________________________

6. ______________________________

8 What are some things you like and don't like about people? Write two sentences about each of the following. Use the ideas in the pictures and your own ideas.

1. What I really like:

I love it when someone
is generous and gives me flowers.
It makes me happy when
____

2. What I don't like:

It bothers me when
____
____
____

3. What doesn't bother me:

I don't mind it when
____
____
____

4. What upsets me:

It upsets me when
____
____
____

9 It really bugs me!

Choose one thing from Exercise 8 that really embarrasses, bothers, or upsets you. Write two paragraphs about it. In the first paragraph, describe the situation. In the second paragraph, say why this situation is difficult for you and describe a situation you would prefer.

It really embarrasses me when someone is too generous to me. Recently, I dated a guy who was always giving me things. For my birthday, he bought me an expensive necklace, and he treated me to dinner and a movie.

The problem is, I don't have enough money to treat him in the same way. I'd prefer to date someone I have more in common with. In fact, my ideal boyfriend is someone who is sensible and saves his money!

____

____

____

____

____

____

____

____

10 Choose the correct word to complete each sentence.

1. I can tell Simon anything, and I know he won't tell anyone else. I can really ____________ him. (believe / treat / trust)
2. Kay has a very high opinion of herself. I don't like people who are so ____________. (egotistical / temperamental / supportive)
3. It bothers me when people are too serious. I prefer people who are ____________ and have a good sense of humor. (easygoing / inflexible / reliable)
4. I like it when someone expresses strong ____________. Hearing other people's views can really make you think. (accomplishments / compliments / opinions)
5. Lisa is very rich, but she only spends her money on herself. She's very ____________. (generous / modest / stingy)

2 Working 9 to 5

1 What's your job?

A Match the jobs with their definitions.

A/An . . .	is a person who . . . .
1. comedian __f__	**a.** researches environmentally friendly technologies
2. green researcher _____	**b.** helps students with their problems
3. guidance counselor _____	**c.** controls a company's brand online
4. organic food farmer _____	**d.** creates computer applications
5. social media manager _____	**e.** grows food without chemicals
6. software developer _____	**f.** makes people laugh for a living

B Write a definition for each of these jobs: accountant, fashion designer, and flight attendant.

1. An accountant is someone who ________________

2. ________________

3. ________________

2 Challenging or frightening?

A Which words have a positive meaning, and which ones have a negative meaning? Write *P* or *N*.

awful __N__
boring _____
challenging _____
dangerous _____
difficult _____
fantastic _____
fascinating _____
frightening _____
interesting _____
rewarding _____

B Write about four more jobs you know. Use the words in part A and gerund phrases.

1. I think being a comedian would be fascinating.

2. ________________

3. ________________

4. ________________

5. ________________

3 Career choices

A Match each career and the most appropriate job responsibility.

Careers		Job responsibilities
work	for an airline	do research
	with computers	teach discipline and fitness
	as a high school coach	learn new software programs
be	a university professor	work independently
	a writer	travel to different countries

B Use the information from part A and gerund phrases to complete this conversation.

Teri: So, what kind of career would you like, Jack?

Jack: Well, I'm not exactly sure. ___Being a writer___ could be interesting. Maybe blogging about something I'm interested in.

Teri: Hmm. I don't know if I'd like that because I'd have to write every day.

Jack: What do you want to do, then?

Teri: Well, I'm not sure either! I'd love ______________________. I'd really enjoy being with teenagers all day and ______________________. On the other hand, I'd be interested in ______________________.

Jack: Really? What would you like about that?

Teri: Well, I'd love ______________________ all over the world.

Jack: Oh, I could never do that! I think it would be very tiring work.

C Write a short conversation like the one in part B. Use the remaining information in part A or your own ideas.

A: So, what kind of career would you like?

B: Well, I'm not exactly sure. ______________________

A: That sounds interesting. But I wouldn't like it because ______________________

B: What do you want to do then?

A: Well, I'd love ______________________

B: ______________________

A: ______________________

4 What a job!

A Read the magazine interviews. Write the correct job title above each interview. There are two extra jobs.

☐ architect	☐ freelance artist	☐ preschool teacher	☐ university professor
☐ bus driver	☐ house painter	☐ train conductor	☐ website designer

TELL US ABOUT YOUR JOB

1 ______________

I have always enjoyed making things, and what's more interesting than building something that people will use for years? The challenge of discovering exactly how a space needs to be constructed for maximum usefulness and beauty is what makes me wake up with a smile. I often work late at the office, but that's part of the job.

2 ______________

Working for yourself is hard because you're responsible for everything. If no one calls you and asks you to work for them, you have to go out and look for work. Luckily, I now have some regular clients. I paint pictures for some expensive hotels. Right now, I'm doing some paintings for the rooms of a new hotel in Hawaii.

3 ______________

My friends say my work is less demanding than theirs, but I work just as hard as they do. I spend a lot of time alone because my job can't begin until all the construction work is completed. Usually, the rooms look great when I've finished my work. Sometimes I don't like the colors that customers choose, but I have to do what they want.

4 ______________

These days a lot of people are doing what I've been doing for fifteen years. I work closely with my clients to find out exactly what they want to show on the Internet and how to make it look as attractive as possible. My work requires a good eye for art, a command of clear and precise language, and of course, knowledge of the latest technology.

5 ______________

I meet all kinds of people: some are the best and others aren't so good. Sometimes I have a great conversation with someone I've never met before. And of course, I have my regulars, people I see every day, and we talk about life. But I always keep my attention on the road.

6 ______________

Being with kids all day isn't for everyone, but I love it. I take care of children when their parents are away. I do all kinds of things – I teach, I play games, and I read books. I make sure the children are safe and happy. I have a lot of responsibility, but I love my job. It's very rewarding work even though the pay isn't great.

B Underline the words and phrases that helped you find the answers in part A.

5 First, use words from the list to complete each job title. Then choose the best expressions to compare the jobs in each sentence.

☐ assistant ☐ counselor ☐ decorator ☐ instructor ☐ painter ☐ ranger ☐ walker ☑ worker

1. A child-care _worker_ doesn't earn _as much as_ an accountant.
   ☑ as much as ☐ greater than ☐ worse than
2. A chef's ______________ has ______________ a waiter.
   ☐ worse hours than ☐ not as good hours ☐ as worse hours as
3. A dog ______________ is ______________ a student intern.
   ☐ more interesting than ☐ not as boring as ☐ better paid than
4. A house ______________ earns ______________ a camp counselor.
   ☐ as bad as ☐ more than ☐ not more than
5. A park ______________ is ______________ a landscaper.
   ☐ as bad as ☐ not as well paid as ☐ worse than
6. Being a yoga ______________ is ______________ being a professor.
   ☐ more than ☐ as much as ☐ not as difficult as
7. Being an interior ______________ is ______________ being a sales assistant.
   ☐ greater than ☐ earns more than ☐ more interesting than
8. A guidance ______________ has ______________ a gardener.
   ☐ more responsibility than ☐ not more than ☐ not as long as

6 Complete these sentences with the correct prepositions. Some of the prepositions may be used more than once. More than one answer may be possible.

☐ as ☐ at ☐ in ☐ on ☐ with

1. Chonglin works ______________ the best Chinese restaurant in Los Angeles.
2. I think working ______________ other people is more fun than working alone.
3. I would hate working ______________ the media. It would be nerve-racking!
4. Working ______________ a dance instructor sounds great.
5. Working ______________ an office is less interesting than working ______________ a cruise ship.

7 Use the words in parentheses to compare the jobs.

Assistant needed at an outdoor swimming pool. Must be able to swim. Responsible for keeping pool and changing rooms clean. $12/hour. Tues.–Fri. 12–7.

Learn web design!
In search of a bright young person to work as an intern for an advertising agency. Some clerical work. $15/hour. Mon.–Fri. 9–5.

1. **A:** An assistant at a swimming pool has shorter hours than an intern.
   (shorter hours)
   B: Yes, but working as an intern is more interesting than being a swimming pool assistant.
   (interesting)

Travel agency needs energetic people. Knowledge of a second language is a plus. Mostly answering the phone. $18/hour. Flexible hours. Five vacation days a year.

Tutors in math, science, English, and music wanted at private summer school. Challenging work with gifted teenagers. Salary negotiable. Mon.–Sat. 3–7.

2. **A:** Working in a ____________
   (better benefits)
   B: Yes, but working ____________
   (challenging)

Tennis instructor needed at summer camp for 12- and 13-year-olds. Must be excellent tennis player and good with kids. $18/hour. Mon.–Fri. 1–7.

Tour company seeks **guide** to lead bus tours. Great attitude and good speaking voice a must! Fun work, but must be willing to work long hours. $15/hour.

3. **A:** ____________
   (make as much money)
   B: ____________
   (work longer hours)

City seeks **taxi drivers** for morning shift. No experience necessary; driver's license required. $15/hour plus tips. Mon.–Thu. 7 A.M.–2 P.M.

Office assistant required in small, friendly office. Computer skills an advantage. Interesting work. Some management skills necessary. $20/hour. 6-day week.

4. **A:** ____________
   (a shorter work week)
   B: ____________
   (less boring)

8 Choose four pairs of jobs from the box below to compare. Say which job you would prefer and give two reasons.

- a graphic designer/a TV news director
- an architect/a teacher
- a guidance counselor/a coach
- a doctor/a musician
- a police officer/a politician
- a secret agent/a psychiatrist
- working on a construction site/working in an office
- being self-employed/working for a company

Example: *Working as a TV news director sounds more interesting than being a graphic designer. A TV news director has more responsibility than a graphic designer. Also, directing the news is better paid.*

1. ______________________________

2. ______________________________

3. ______________________________

4. ______________________________

3 Lend a hand.

1 Would you mind . . . ?

A Complete the request for each situation.

1. You want to borrow a classmate's pen.
   Can I borrow your pen?
2. You want a classmate to give you a ride home after class.
   Would you mind ______________________
3. You want to turn down your roommate's TV.
   Is it OK if ______________________
4. You want to use a friend's cell phone.
   Do you mind if ______________________
5. You want to borrow a friend's car for the weekend.
   I was wondering if ______________________
6. You want someone to tell you how to get to the subway.
   Could ______________________

B Think of four more things you would need to have done if you were going on a long vacation. Write requests asking a friend to do the things.

1. *Could you water the plants?*
2. ______________________
3. ______________________
4. ______________________
5. ______________________

2 Accept or decline these requests. For requests you decline, give excuses. Use the expressions in the chart or expressions of your own.

Accepting	Declining
That's OK, I guess.	Sorry, but . . .
I'd be glad to.	I'd like to, but . . .
Fine. No problem.	Unfortunately, . . .

1. **A:** Can I use your computer? My computer crashed.
   B: *Sorry, but I'm going to use it myself in a few minutes.*
2. **A:** I've just finished this ten-page paper. Could you check it for me, please?
   B: ______
3. **A:** I was wondering if I could stay at your place for a week while my landlord fixes the roof.
   B: ______
4. **A:** Would you mind if I used your cell phone to make a long-distance call to Nigeria?
   B: ______

3 Look at the pictures and write the conversations. Speaker A makes a request. Speaker B declines it. Each speaker should give a reason.

1. **A:** *Could you carry these boxes for me? I have a bad back.*
   B: *Sorry, but I have a bad back, too.*
   ______

2. **A:** ______
   ______
   B: ______
   ______

3. **A:** ______
   ______
   B: ______
   ______

4 Getting what you want

A Scan the magazine article about making requests. What strategies can you use for less formal requests? What strategies can you use for more formal requests?

The Art of Making Requests

When you make a request, it helps to be clear about two things: Firstly, how well do you know the other person? Secondly, how important is it for you to get what you want? Are you willing to take "no" for an answer?

Let's say that you would like to borrow someone's car to go out on Friday night. Because borrowing a car is a big favor, we can assume that you'd probably only ask someone you know well for this favor. In general, when making requests of friends or close acquaintances, you can use a less formal approach.

Now let's imagine that it's very important for you to have that car on Friday night; you have to have it. In that case, you can let the other person know in a less formal, direct way. Here are two possible strategies:

1. Make a statement with *need*: "I need to borrow your car."
2. Use an imperative: "Please lend me your car."

By avoiding questions, this approach makes it more difficult for the other person to say no. If you are willing to put the other person in a possibly awkward situation, then this is definitely the clearest, and perhaps most effective, way of getting what you want.

But maybe you expect the other person to say no, and you can live with that. This attitude allows you to have a cooler, more objective perspective, so you can make your request in a more formal, indirect way.

Here are some examples:

3. Ask about ability: "Could/Can you lend me your car?"
4. Be polite – use *may*: "May I borrow your car?"
5. Ask for permission: "Would it be OK if I borrowed your car?"
6. Express curiosity: "I wonder if I could borrow your car."
7. State the request negatively: "I don't suppose you could lend me your car."
8. Apologize: "I hope you don't mind my asking, but could I borrow your car?"
9. Give a hint: "I have plans for Friday night, but I don't have a car."

This approach gives the other person a polite way to refuse if, for any reason, they don't want to or cannot lend you their car. And even though you know the person well, taking a more formal approach proves to the listener that you realize what a big favor you're asking. It shows them respect and appreciation – which makes it more likely that you'll get the result you want!

B Read the article. Check (✓) if each request is less formal or more formal. Then write the correct number from the article (1–9) for each type of request. Only eight of the numbers will be used.

	Less formal	More formal	Type
1. Close the door.	☐	☐	____
2. It's really cold in here.	☐	☐	____
3. Could you possibly move your car?	☐	☐	____
4. May I borrow your dictionary?	☐	☐	____
5. I was wondering if you could help me with this assignment.	☐	☐	____
6. I need some help moving to my new apartment.	☐	☐	____
7. I'm sorry, but I can't stand loud music.	☐	☐	____
8. I don't suppose I could borrow your camera.	☐	☐	____

5 Nouns and verbs

A Complete this chart. Then check your answers in a dictionary.

Noun	Verb	Noun	Verb
apology	*apologize*	invitation	______
compliment	______	permission	______
explanation	______	request	______

B Check (✓) the phrase that describes what each person is doing.

1. Don't worry. I know you didn't mean to break it.
- ☐ returning a favor
- ☐ accepting an apology

2. I really like your new haircut.
- ☐ giving a reason
- ☐ giving a compliment

3. Can I borrow your laptop?
- ☐ asking for a favor
- ☐ giving a gift

4. I can't lend you my bike because I need it myself.
- ☐ declining a request
- ☐ accepting an invitation

5. Could you help me cook dinner?
- ☐ making a request
- ☐ returning a compliment

6 Choose the correct words.

1. My phone didn't work for a week. The phone company ______________ an apology and took $20 off my bill. (accepted / denied / offered)

2. A friend of mine really loves to ______________ compliments, but he never gives anyone else one. I don't understand why he's like that. (do / owe / receive)

3. Diane is always talking on the phone. She makes a lot of calls, but she rarely ______________ mine. Maybe she never listens to her voice mail! (makes / offers / returns)

4. I need to ______________ a favor. Could you please give me a ride to school tomorrow? My bike has a flat tire! (ask for / give / turn down)

7 Use these messages to complete the phone conversations. Use indirect requests.

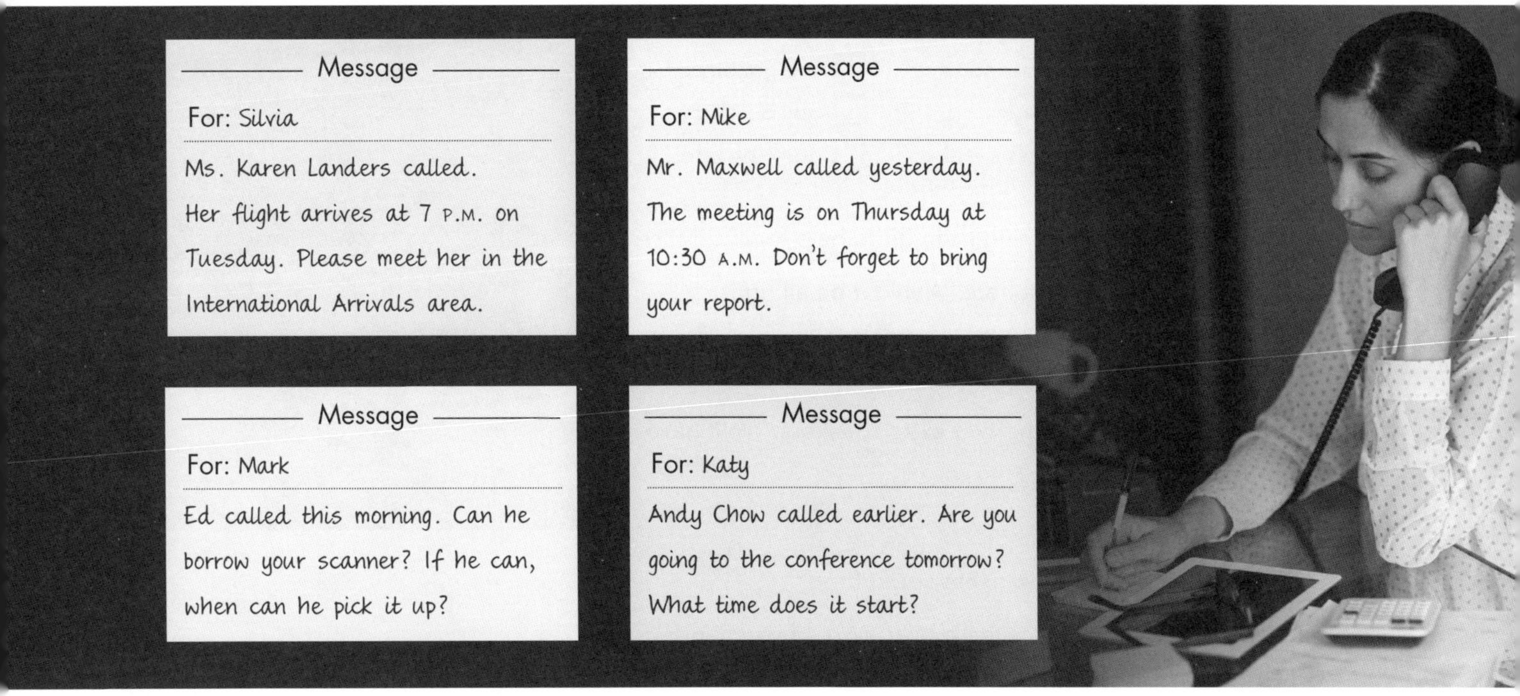

1. **A:** Is Silvia Vega there, please?
   B: No, she isn't. Would you like to leave a message?
   A: Yes, please. This is Karen Landers calling from Toronto.
   Could you tell her *that my flight arrives at 7 P.M. on Tuesday* ____________________?
   Would ____________________?
   B: OK, I'll give her the message.
2. **A:** Can I speak to Mark, please?
   B: I'm afraid he's not here. Do you want to leave a message?
   A: Yes, please. This is Ed. Please ____________________.
   And if it's OK, could you ____________________?
   B: Sure, I'll leave him the message.
3. **A:** Could I speak to Mike, please?
   B: I'm sorry, but he's not here right now.
   A: Oh, OK. This is Mr. Maxwell. I'd like to leave a message.
   Could ____________________?
   Could ____________________?
4. **A:** I'd like to speak to Katy, please.
   B: She's not here right now. Can I take a message?
   A: Yeah. This is Andy Chow.
   Can ____________________?
   And would ____________________?
   B: OK, I'll give Katy your message.

8 Complete the conversation with the information in the box. Add any words necessary and use the correct form of the verbs given.

☐ ask Kelly to get some soda	☐ bring a big salad
☐ borrow some money	☐ buy dessert
☑ borrow your wireless speaker	☐ don't be late

Dan: So, is there anything I can do to help for the party?

Mark: Yeah. I have a list here. Would it be all right *if I borrowed your wireless speaker* ? Mine isn't working very well.

Dan: Sure. And I'll bring two extra speakers. We'll have amazing sound.

Mark: Thanks.

Dan: No problem. Now, what about food?

Mark: Well, I thought maybe a salad. Would you mind ______________________, too?

Dan: Well, OK. And how about drinks?

Mark: Well, could you ______________________? And please tell her ______________________. Last time we had a party, she didn't arrive till eleven o'clock, and everyone got really thirsty!

Dan: I remember.

Mark: One more thing – I was wondering if you could ______________________.

Dan: Um, sure. All right. But, uh, would you mind if I ______________________ to pay for it?

9 Rewrite these sentences. Find another way to say each sentence using the words given.

1. Can I use your cell phone?
   Would it be OK if I used your cell phone? (OK)
2. Please ask Annie to stop by and talk to me.
   ______________________ (would)
3. Could I borrow your guitar?
   ______________________ (wonder)
4. Would you ask Mitch what time he's coming over?
   ______________________ (could / when)
5. Lend me your hairbrush.
   ______________________ (mind)

4 What happened?

1 Complete these news stories using the verbs from the box.

1.

☐ broke	☐ found	☐ locking	☐ stayed	☑ went
☐ drank	☐ heard	☐ shouted	☐ waiting	☐ wondered

WOMAN TRAPPED IN BATHROOM FOR 20 DAYS

A 69-year-old grandmother in Paris ___went___ to the bathroom – and ______________ there for twenty days. What happened? As she was ______________ the door, the lock ______________. She could not open the door. She ______________ for help, but no one ______________ her because her bathroom had no windows. After nearly three weeks, the woman's neighbors ______________ where she was. Firefighters broke into her apartment and ______________ her in a "very weakened" state. While she was ______________ to be rescued, she ______________ warm water.

2.

☐ became	☐ checking in	☐ entered	☐ opened	☐ sleeping
☐ behaving	☐ decided	☐ had	☐ showed	

TIGER CUB FOUND IN LUGGAGE

A woman was ______________ strangely when she ______________ the Bangkok airport. While she was ______________ for an overseas flight, she ______________ difficulty with a very large bag. The check-in clerk ______________ suspicious and ______________ to X-ray the bag. The X-ray ______________ an image that looked like an animal. When airport staff ______________ the bag, they saw that a baby tiger was ______________ under lots of toy tigers. The tiger was taken to a rescue center for wildlife, and the woman was arrested.

2 Join each sentence in column A with an appropriate sentence in column B. Use *as*, *when*, or *while* to join the sentences.

A	B
I was crossing the road.	My racket broke.
I was using my computer.	A car nearly hit me.
We were playing tennis.	The water got cold.
I was taking a shower.	I burned my finger.
I was cooking dinner.	It suddenly stopped working.

1. As I was crossing the road, a car nearly hit me.
2. ______________________________
3. ______________________________
4. ______________________________
5. ______________________________

3 Complete these conversations. Use the simple past or the past continuous of the verbs given.

1. **A:** Guess what happened to me last night! As I __was getting__ (get) into bed, I ______________ (hear) a loud noise like a gunshot in the street. Then the phone ______________ (ring).
   B: Who was it?
   A: It was Luisa. She always calls me late at night, but this time she had a reason. She ______________ (drive) right past my apartment when she ______________ (get) a flat tire. It was very late, so while we ______________ (change) the tire, I ______________ (invite) her to spend the night.
2. **A:** I'm sorry I'm so late, Erin. I was at the dentist.
   B: Don't tell me! While you ______________ (sit) in the waiting room, you ______________ (meet) someone interesting. I know how you are, Matt!
   A: Well, you're wrong this time. The dentist ______________ (clean) my teeth when she suddenly ______________ (get) called away for an emergency. So I just sat there waiting for two hours with my mouth hanging open!

4 Lost and found

A Read this news story. Who is it about? Where did it take place?

Thank you, Andre Botha!

On December 6, 2015, Andre Botha was in the water, watching the big waves at the Pipeline off the island of Oahu, Hawaii, when he noticed something strange. The two-time world bodyboarding champion realized that professional champion surfer Evan Geiselman was in big trouble. Since the Pipeline has some of the biggest waves in the world and is considered to be the most dangerous place on the planet for surfing, situations like this are, unfortunately, not uncommon.

Surfing at the Pipeline

Botha realized that the surfer, who had entered the inside of a huge wave and was riding it, was knocked off his surfboard when the wave crashed on him. Normally a surfer will come up to the surface of the water a few moments after falling off the board. But there was no sign of Geiselman. Botha began to swim on his bodyboard as fast as he could to where the surfboard was being thrown around by the huge waves. When he reached the surfboard, he saw Geiselman, who looked like he might be dead. The surfer was unconscious and his face was turning blue as Botha tried to bring him back to life in the water. Botha breathed into Geiselman's mouth and hit him on the chest to get him breathing again. Then he began to swim to shore with the surfer's unconscious body. Two lifeguards swam out to meet him, and they brought Geiselman to a hospital.

Bodyboarding

Surfers and bodyboarders agree that Evan Geiselman would probably not be alive today if Andre Botha had not rescued him. They don't always agree about which sport is best, but surfers and bodyboarders do agree that taking care of each other in the big waves is important. This respect and care for people is a wonderful part of these exciting sports.

B Use the article to answer these questions.

1. In what sport is Andre Botha a two-time champion?

   ____

2. What sport does Evan Geiselman excel at as a champion?

   ____

3. Where is the Pipeline located?

   ____

4. What is one way you can help an unconscious person start breathing?

   ____

5. Who brought Geiselman to the hospital?

   ____

6. What helps make bodyboarding and surfing such wonderful sports?

   ____

5 Think of a real or imaginary problem like the one in Exercise 4. Write two paragraphs. In the first paragraph, describe your problem. In the second, say how you solved it.

____
____
____
____
____
____
____
____
____
____
____

A couple of years ago, I got lost in the mountains. I was hiking when it suddenly got foggy. I was really frightened because I couldn't see anything, and it was getting cold. I decided to put up my tent and stay there for the night.

While I was putting up my tent, though, the fog began to clear. . . .

6 Choose the correct verbs to complete the story.

Grammar note: *After*

In sentences using *after* that show one past event occurring before another, the clause with *after* usually uses the past perfect.

After she **had called** her friend, her cell phone battery died.

Andy and I ___had just gotten___ (just got / had just gotten) engaged, so we went to a jewelry store to buy a wedding ring. We ______________ (just chose / had just chosen) a ring when a masked man ______________ (came in / had come in). After the robber ______________ (took / had taken) Andy's wallet, he ______________ (demanded / had demanded) the ring. I ______________ (just handed / had just handed) it to him when the alarm ______________ (started / had started) to go off, and the robber ______________ (ran off / had run off). We were so relieved! But then the sales assistant ______________ (told / had told) us we had to pay for the ring because I ______________ (gave / had given) it to the robber. We ______________ (just told / had just told) her that we wouldn't pay for it when the police ______________ (arrived / had arrived) and ______________ (arrested / had arrested) us! What a terrible experience!

7 What a story!

A Choose the best headline for each of these news stories.

What a disaster! | **What a triumph!** | **What an emergency!** | **What a lucky break!** | **What a dilemma!**

1. ______________________

Karen Lane was seven months pregnant when she and her husband, Scott, went on vacation to a small **remote** island off the coast of South America. On the first night, Karen was in a lot of pain. There were no doctors on the island, so Scott called a hospital on the **mainland**. They told him they could not send a helicopter because a typhoon was coming. During the night, Karen thought she was going to die. Luckily, the typhoon had passed over the island by the following morning. A helicopter picked Karen up and took her to the hospital – just in time for her to have a beautiful baby girl.

2. ______________________

Serena Mills was very sick for several months before her final exams this summer. She couldn't study at all. Her parents suggested she should **skip** a year and take the exams the next summer. **Remarkably**, Serena suddenly got well just before the exams, spent two weeks studying, and got the highest grade in her class!

3. ______________________

Mark Blaine had waited years for a **promotion**. Finally, a week ago, he was offered the position he had always wanted – Regional Manager. On the same day, however, he won $6 million in the lottery. Mark's wife wants him to **resign** from his job and take her on a trip around the world. Mark says he cannot decide what to do.

B Look at the words in bold in the articles. What do you think they mean?

remote ______________ skip ______________ promotion ______________

mainland ______________ remarkably ______________ resign ______________

8 Complete the sentences. Use the simple past, the past continuous, or the past perfect of the verbs given.

1. In 2011, two divers ___*discovered*___ (discover) the remains of a 200-year-old shipwreck while they ______________ (dive) off the coast of Rhode Island, in the eastern United States.
2. After an art show ______________ (open) in New York, it was discovered that someone ______________ (hang) a famous painting by Henri Matisse upside down.
3. In 2015, workers ______________ (find) a chemistry lab from the 1840s while they ______________ (repair) a building at the University of Virginia in the United States. The lab was behind a wall of the current building.
4. Chile's Calbuco volcano ______________ (surprise) residents of Santiago when it erupted in 2015. Before that, an eruption of Calbuco ______________ (not happen) for over 40 years.

9 Read this situation. Then use the information and clues to complete the chart. Write the name of each reporter and each country. (You will leave one square in the chart blank.)

Five news reporters – two women and three men – arrived for an international conference on Sunday, Monday, and Tuesday.

No more than two people came on the same day. The reporters came from five different countries.

Clues

The women: Ms. Johnson and Ms. Marshall

The men: Mr. James, Mr. Grant, and Mr. Simpson

The countries: Australia, Mexico, Brazil, Singapore, and the United States

The arrivals:

- Mr. Simpson arrived late at night. No one else had arrived that day.
- Ms. Johnson and Mr. Grant arrived on the same day.
- The man who came from Singapore had arrived the day before.
- The reporters who came from Brazil and Australia arrived on the same day.
- Mr. James and the woman who came from Brazil arrived on Tuesday, after Mr. Grant.
- The reporter from Australia arrived the day after the person who came from the United States.
- Mr. Grant came from North America but not the United States.

Reporters' countries and arrival days		
Sunday	Name: ________ Country: ________	Name: ________ Country: ________
Monday	Name: ________ Country: ________	Name: ________ Country: ________
Tuesday	Name: ________ Country: ________	Name: ________ Country: ________

5 Expanding your horizons

1 Complete these sentences. Use words from the box.

☐ confident	☐ depressed	☐ fascinated	☐ uncomfortable
☐ curious	☑ embarrassed	☐ uncertain	☐ worried

1. In my country, people never leave tips. So when I first went abroad, I kept forgetting to tip servers. I felt really __*embarrassed*__.
2. The first time I traveled abroad, I felt really ________________. I was alone, I didn't speak the language, and I didn't make any friends.
3. I just spent a year in France learning to speak French. It was a satisfying experience, and I was ________________ by the culture.
4. At first I really didn't like shopping in the open-air markets. I felt ________________ because so many people were trying to sell me something at the same time.
5. When I arrived in Lisbon, I was nervous because I couldn't speak any Portuguese. As I began to learn the language, though, I became more ________________ about living there.
6. Before I went to Alaska last winter, I was very ________________ about the cold. But it wasn't a problem because most buildings there are well heated.
7. When I was traveling in Southeast Asia, I couldn't believe how many different kinds of fruit there were. I was ________________ to try all of them, so I ate a lot of fruit!
8. It was our first trip to Latin America, so we were ________________ about what to expect. We loved it and hope to return again soon.

2 Imagine you are going to travel to a country you have never visited before. Write sentences using the factors and feelings given. Then add another sentence explaining your feelings.

Factors	Feelings
public transportation	anxious (about)
shopping	comfortable (with)
the climate	curious (about)
the food	enthusiastic (about)
the language	fascinated (by)
the money	nervous (about)
the music	uncertain (about)
the people my age	uncomfortable (with)

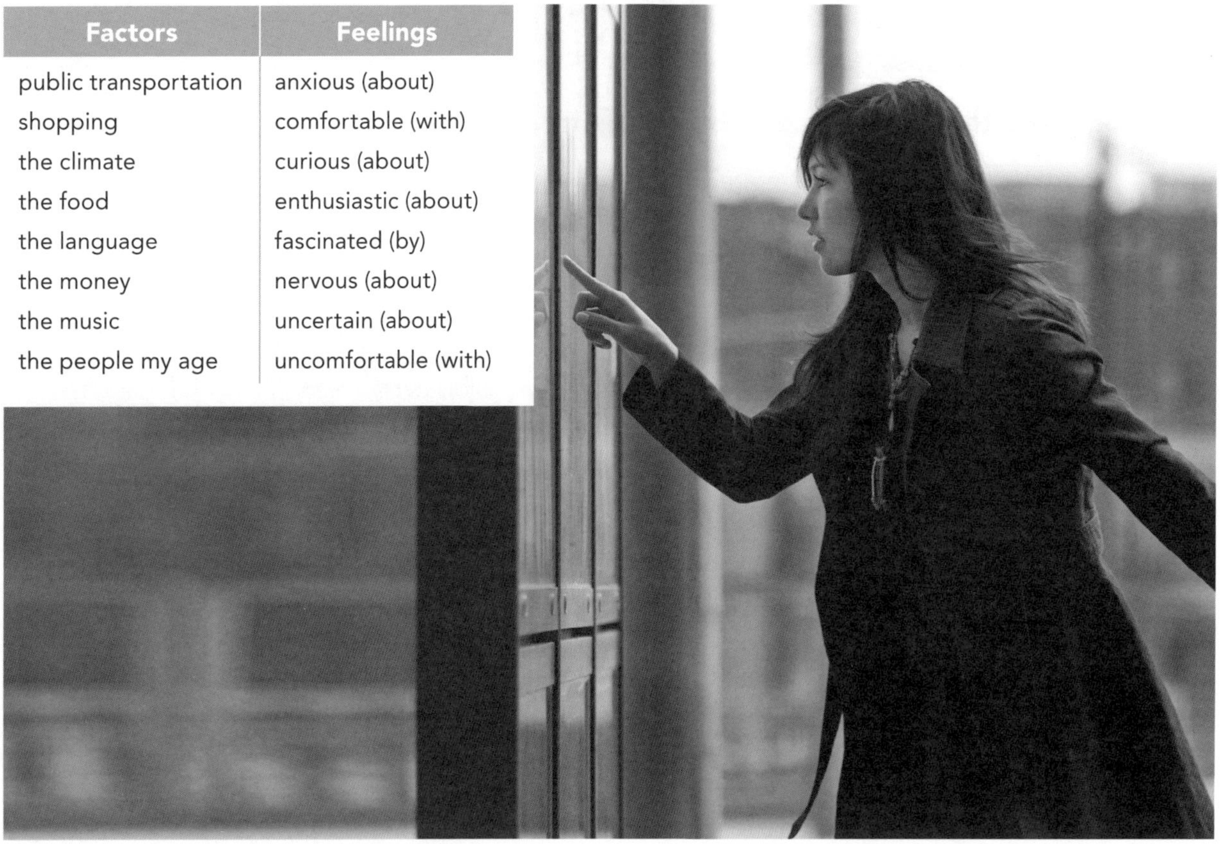

1. *Public transportation is something I'd be anxious about. I'd be afraid of getting lost.*
2.
3.
4.
5.
6.
7.
8.
9.

3 Culture shock!

A Make a list of four pieces of advice to help people feel comfortable about traveling abroad.

B Scan the article about cultural differences. Where can you find articles like this? Who was it written for?

Culture Shock

Each society has its own beliefs, attitudes, customs, behaviors, and social habits. These things give people a sense of who they are and how they are supposed to behave.

People become conscious of such rules when they meet people from different cultures. For example, the rules about when to eat vary from culture to culture. Many North Americans and Europeans organize their timetables around three mealtimes a day. In other countries, however, it's not the custom to have strict rules like this – people eat when they want to, and every family has its own timetable.

When people visit or live in a country for the first time, they are often surprised at the differences between this culture and the culture in their own country. For some people, traveling abroad is the thing they enjoy most in life; for others, cultural differences make them feel uncomfortable, frightened, and insecure. This is known as "culture shock."

When you're visiting a foreign country, it is important to understand and appreciate cultural differences. This can help you avoid misunderstandings, develop friendships more easily, and feel more comfortable when traveling or living abroad.

Here are several things to do in order to avoid culture shock.

1 Instead of criticizing, enjoy the new customs you discover each day on your trip as much as possible.

2 If you read or understand the language, read a local newspaper or listen to the radio to find out what news they're likely to be talking about.

3 Talk to people in order to understand their ideas about their own country as well as their thoughts about yours.

4 Remember the proverb, "When in Rome, do as the Romans do." It's a great way to start learning new things!

5 For instance, try one new thing every day, like a food you've never had before, instead of choosing something on the menu that you can have in your own country.

6 Read a book about the history of the place you are in so you will understand it better while you are there.

7 Go to concerts, museums, theatrical performances, and sporting events to appreciate the culture of this country.

8 Remember that traveling is an educational experience, so be ready to question the stereotypes you may have of another country, and learn about the stereotypes people in that country may have about the place you come from.

C Read the article. Use your own words to write definitions for these words.

1. culture ______________________________

2. culture shock ______________________________

3. appreciate ______________________________

4. stereotypes ______________________________

D After reading the article, would you make any changes to the pieces of advice you listed in part A?

4 Complete these sentences by giving information about customs in a country you know.

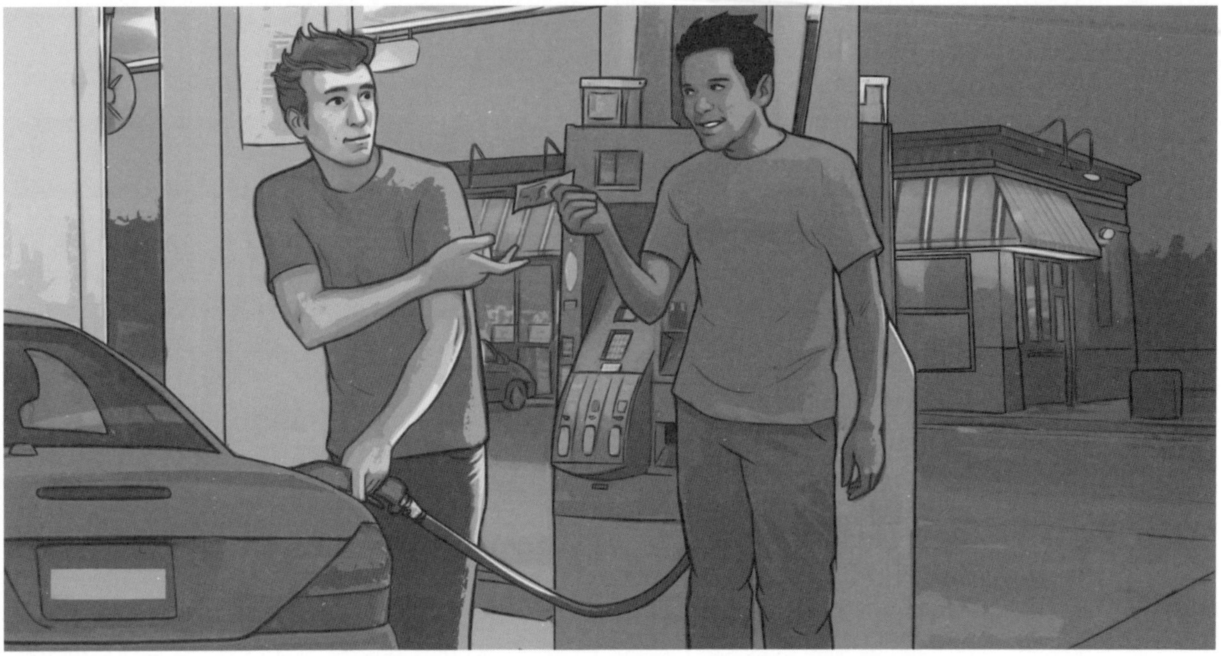

1. If you go for a long ride in a friend's car, *it's the custom to offer to pay for some of the expenses.*
2. When a friend graduates from school or college, ______________________________
____
3. If you borrow something from a friend, ______________________________
____
4. When a friend invites you to dinner, ______________________________
____

5 Contrasting customs

A Read the information about the different customs and find four pairs of countries with contrasting customs. Write the countries on the lines below.

Country	Custom
Brazil	Friends kiss each other three or four times on the cheeks as a greeting.
Denmark	People generally arrive on time for most occasions.
Egypt	People allow their hosts to treat them to meals in restaurants.
France	Service is usually included in the price of a meal in restaurants.
Japan	People bow when they see or meet someone they know.
New Zealand	People usually pay for their own meals in restaurants.
Spain	People usually arrive late for most appointments.
United States	People leave a tip of 15–20 percent in restaurants.

1. *Brazil and Japan*
2. ______________________________
3. ______________________________
4. ______________________________

B Read these five cross-cultural situations. Write sentences describing what the visitors did wrong. Use the expressions in the box.

you're (not) supposed to
you're (not) expected to
it's (not) the custom to
it's (not) acceptable to

1. Enni is from Denmark. When she was on vacation in Spain, some Spanish friends invited her to dinner at 9:00. She arrived at exactly 9:00, but her friends had not even arrived home yet.

   In Spain, you're expected to ______________________

   ____

2. Kayla is from the United States. During her first week in Paris, she went to a restaurant with some new friends. She was so happy with the service that she left a tip of 20 percent. Her friends were a little embarrassed.

   In France, ______________________

   ____

3. James is from New Zealand. When he went to Egypt, he was invited to dinner at a restaurant. When the bill came, he offered to pay for his dinner. His Egyptian friend was kind of upset.

   In Egypt, ______________________

   ____

4. Clara is from Brazil. She was working for a year in Osaka, Japan. One day, when she saw a Japanese co-worker in a bookstore, she went to say hello and kissed him on the cheeks. Her friend was very surprised.

   ____

   ____

5. Brian is from Canada. He was on vacation in Bali, Indonesia, and some new friends invited him to a temple to watch a special dance performance. He arrived on time wearing a clean T-shirt and shorts, but they said he couldn't go inside the temple because he wasn't dressed properly.

   ____

   ____

6 Complete these sentences with information about yourself (1–4) and about a country you know well (5–8).

1. One reason I'd feel homesick abroad is ______
2. Something that would fascinate me would be ______
3. Traveling alone is something ______
4. Getting used to hot weather is one thing ______
5. In ______, it's the custom to ______
6. If you have good service in a restaurant, ______
7. You're expected to ______ when ______
8. It's just not acceptable to ______ if ______

7 Write about living in a foreign country. In the first paragraph, write about two things you would enjoy. In the second paragraph, write about two things you might worry about.

6 That needs fixing.

1 What's wrong with it?

A What can be wrong with these things? Put these words in the correct categories. (Most words go in more than one category.)

bike blouse car carpet chair glasses plate sink tablecloth

chipped	cracked	dented	leaking	scratched	stained	torn

B What is wrong with these things? Use the words in part A to write a sentence about each one.

1. *The car is scratched.* OR *There's a scratch on the car.*

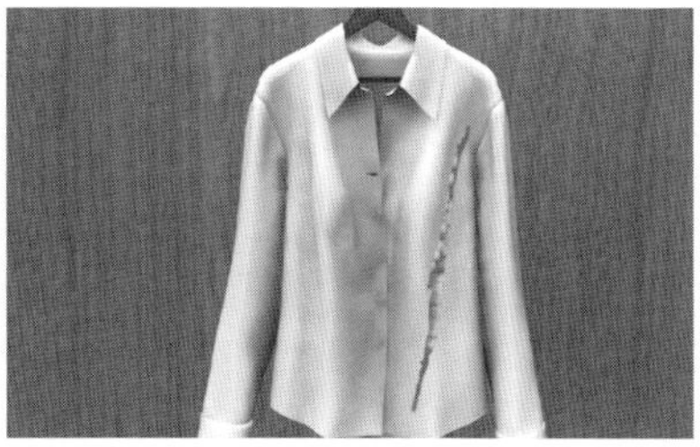

2. ______________________________

3. ______________________________

4. ______________________________

5. ______________________________

6. ______________________________

7. ______________________________

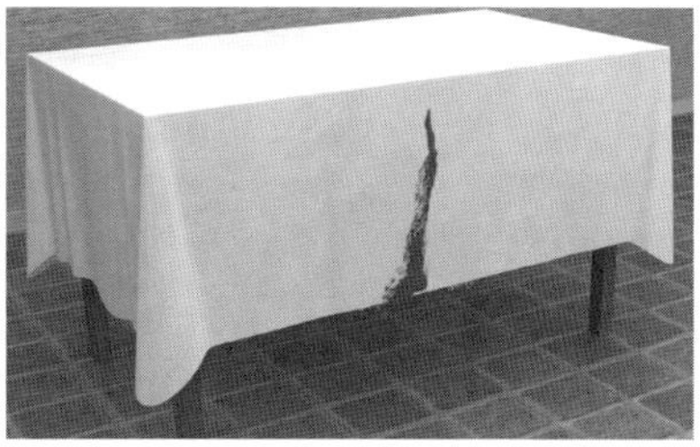

8. ______________________________

9. ______________________________

2 Problems, problems, problems!

A Scan the articles in *Consumer* magazine. Who would read articles like these? Why?

George's Class Trip

George Humphrey is a Spanish teacher at Crockett College in Duluth, Minnesota. Last year, George took his summer class from Duluth to Madrid, Spain. At the end of the six-week trip, George and the twenty students had a delayed flight at the airport in Madrid when they were coming home. Because of the six-hour delay in Madrid, they missed their plane from New York to Minnesota. Everyone had to stay at a hotel in New York City, and they all spent a lot more money than they had expected. They were also more than 24 hours late when they finally got back to Duluth. When George asked the airline office in New York to pay for their hotel and restaurant bills, the airline refused.

George contacted *Consumer* magazine. We talked to a representative of the airline office in Madrid and discovered that, in Europe, airlines must pay for delays – but that does not apply to airlines in the U.S. However, because the delay first occurred in Madrid, George and each student received 400 euros. George was very pleased, especially for his students. In his email to us, George wrote that he believes the law regarding airline delays needs changing in the U.S.

Diane's Vacation

Diane Gleason is a clothing designer in Cincinnati, Ohio. For her vacation last year, she decided to go somewhere she had never been – the southwestern part of the U.S. When she arrived at the airport in Phoenix, Arizona, she rented a beautiful red convertible for her trip. She planned to drive from Phoenix to the Grand Canyon to go hiking with friends for a few days. After she left the airport, Diane spent the night in Phoenix. The next morning, Diane discovered that someone had stolen the car from the parking lot. She called the car-rental agency, and they told her she was responsible for the cost of the car because she had left the keys in it. They would not let her rent another car until she paid for the stolen one. Diane didn't know what to do. She went back to the motel and contacted *Consumer* magazine.

We called the rental agency, and they told us that Diane had not bought special insurance for a stolen car. We told the agency that Diane needed help: she was all alone and feeling worried and depressed about what happened. The agency suggested that we contact Diane's credit card company. We did, and they told us that Diane was protected because of her credit card. They would pay for the stolen car! By evening, Diane had rented another car from the same agency and, that night, she had dinner at the Grand Canyon with her friends.

B Read the articles and complete the chart. Did George and Diane receive money?

	Problems	What *Consumer* magazine did	Received money? Yes	No
1. George's trip	delay in Madrid __________ __________	__________ __________ __________	☐	☐
2. Diane's vacation	__________ __________ __________	__________ __________ __________	☐	☐

3 Choose appropriate verbs to complete the sentences. Use passive infinitives (*to be* + past participle) or gerunds.

Language note: Verbs ending in -*en* or -*n*

Some verbs are formed by adding -*en* or -*n* to a noun or adjective.
These verbs mean "to make more of something."

Noun		**Verb**	**Adjective**		**Verb**
length	→	length**en**	loose	→	loose**n**
(make something longer)			(make something looser)		

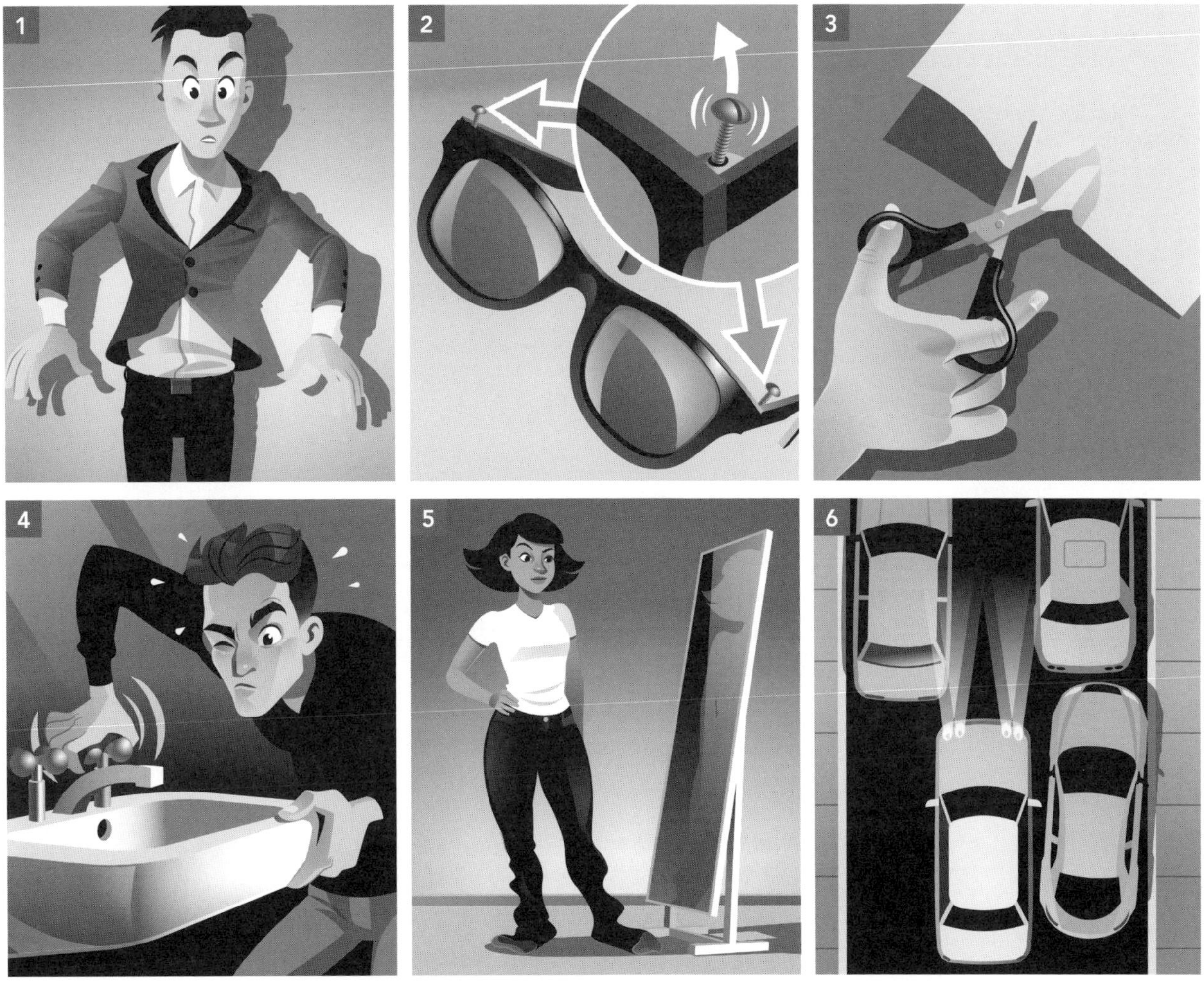

☑ lengthen ☐ loosen ☐ sharpen ☐ shorten ☐ tighten ☐ widen

1. This jacket is too short.
   It needs to be lengthened. OR
   It needs lengthening.
2. The screws on these glasses are too loose.
   They need ______________________
3. The blades on these scissors are too dull.
   They need ______________________
4. This faucet is too tight.
   It needs ______________________
5. These pants are too long.
   They need ______________________
6. This street is too narrow.
   It needs ______________________

4 Complete the conversation. Use *keep, keeps, need,* or *needs* with passive infinitives or gerunds of the verbs given.

Jack: Guess what? Someone broke into my car last night!

Mia: Oh, no. What did they take?

Jack: Nothing! But they did a lot of damage. The lock *needs to be repaired* (repair). And the window ________________ (replace).

Mia: It was probably some young kids having "fun."

Jack: Yeah, some fun. I think they had a party in my car! The seats ________________ (clean).

Mia: How annoying. Does the car drive OK?

Jack: No, it feels strange. The gears ________________ (stick), so they ________________ (fix). And the brakes ________________ (check) right away.

Mia: Well, I guess you're lucky they didn't steal it!

Jack: Yeah, lucky me.

5 Write about something you bought that had something wrong with it. In the first paragraph, describe the problem. In the second paragraph, explain what you did about it.

> Recently, I bought an espresso machine. While I was unpacking it, I could see it was already damaged. The glass carafe was chipped and needed to be replaced. And to make matters worse, the machine leaked!
>
> I took it back to the store. I was worried because the machine had been on sale, and I had lost my receipt. Luckily, the clerk didn't ask me for it. She said a lot of customers had recently had the same problem, and she gave me a better machine at the same price.

____

____

____

____

____

____

____

____

____

____

6 Paul will fix it!

A Match each problem with the repair needed.

PAUL'S REPAIR SHOP

ITEM	PROBLEM	REPAIR NEEDED
1. dishwasher	doesn't work __f__	a. tighten and glue the legs
2. DVD player	DVD is stuck _____	b. repair the wire
3. speakers	wire is damaged _____	c. remove the DVD
4. dresser	mirror is cracked _____	d. repaint the door
5. stove	metal door is scratched _____	e. replace the mirror
6. table	legs are loose _____	f. check the motor

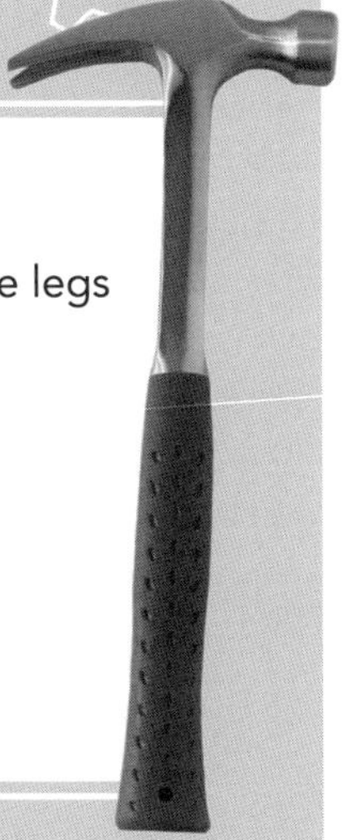

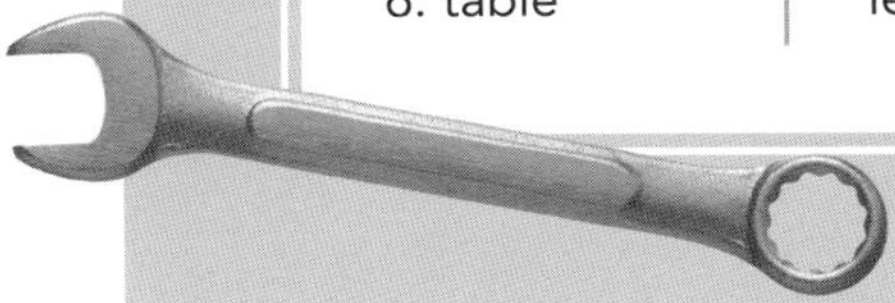

B Write a sentence describing each problem. Then add a sentence describing the action needed to fix it. Use passive infinitives or gerunds.

1. *The dishwasher doesn't work. The motor needs to be checked.* OR
The motor needs checking.
2. ______________________________
3. ______________________________
4. ______________________________
5. ______________________________
6. ______________________________

C Think of three items you own that are damaged (or were damaged) in some way. Write a sentence describing each problem. Then write another sentence describing the action needed to fix it.

1. ______________________________
2. ______________________________
3. ______________________________

7 Complete the sentences with the correct forms of the words in the box.

☐ chip	☑ drop	☐ freeze	☐ scratch
☐ clean	☐ fix	☐ jam	☐ stick
☐ die	☐ flicker	☐ leak	☐ torn

1. This cell phone is driving me crazy! My calls keep ___dropping___.
2. Your computer screen is so dirty. It needs to be ______________.
3. Something is wrong with your TV screen. It keeps ______________. It's time to get a new one.
4. I hate this printer. It keeps ______________. The copies won't come out.
5. Be careful – your cup is ______________. I don't want you to cut yourself.
6. The buttons on this remote control keep ______________. Do you have something to clean it with?
7. Do you realize your jeans are ______________ in the back?
8. Your bathroom faucet keeps ______________. Do you want me to try to fix it?
9. My new glasses already have a ______________ on one of the lenses. How did that happen?
10. Did your laptop ______________ again? I find that so annoying.
11. This old scanner doesn't work at all anymore. It needs to be ______________.
12. The battery in my cell phone keeps ______________. I should buy a new one.

7 What can we do?

1 Use the information in the pamphlet and the verbs and prepositions given below to change the sentences from the active to the passive.

HERE ARE JUST SOME OF THE DANGERS FACING YOU AND YOUR CHILDREN.

The water we drink

1. Agricultural runoff is contaminating the water supply.
2. Chlorine and other additives have ruined the taste of our drinking water.

The food we eat

3. Certain agricultural pesticides have caused new illnesses.
4. Pollution from cars and trucks is destroying our crops.

The air we breathe

5. Factories are releasing dangerous chemicals.
6. Breathing smog every day has damaged many people's health.

The world we live in

7. The lack of rainfall has created more severe droughts.
8. Global warming is threatening our forests and wildlife.

Join **Save Our Planet** today!

1. *The water supply is being contaminated due to agricultural runoff.* (due to)
2. ______________________________ (by)
3. ______________________________ (by)
4. ______________________________ (because of)
5. ______________________________ (by)
6. ______________________________ (as a result of)
7. ______________________________ (through)
8. ______________________________ (by)

2 Verbs and nouns

A Complete the chart.

Verb	Noun	Verb	Noun
contaminate	contamination	educate	________
contribute	________	________	pollution
________	creation	populate	________
deplete	________	protect	________
________	destruction	________	reduction

B Write four sentences like the ones in Exercise 1 using words from the chart.

Example: Many rivers and streams have been badly contaminated by industrial waste.

1. ____
2. ____
3. ____
4. ____

3 Choose the correct words or phrases.

1. Green organizations are trying to save rain forests that have been threatened by developers and farmers. (created / ruined / threatened)
2. One way to inform the public about factories that pollute the environment is through ____________ programs on TV. (agricultural / educational / industrial)
3. In many countries around the world, threatened animal and plant species are being ____________ by strict laws. (created / polluted / protected)
4. Agricultural pesticides are ____________ the soil in many countries. (damaging / eating up / lowering)
5. ____________ is an enormous problem in many large cities where whole families can only afford to live in one room. (pollution / poverty / waste)

El Yunque rain forest

4 How safe is the fleece you are wearing?

A Scan the title and first two paragraphs of this article. What is fleece? Do you own clothing made of fleece? What clothing?

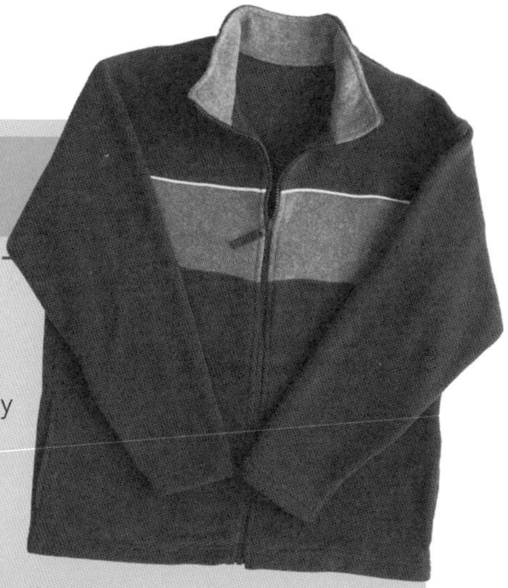

The Fleece that Came to Dinner

Today, half of the clothing bought by people is made of a synthetic fiber. And that figure is almost 70% in the developing world. Synthetics – or fibers that are created by science, not by nature – are very attractive to customers because, for example, some of them are water-resistant, which is particularly desirable for rain gear and hiking shoes. Moreover, synthetics don't require the amount of water, labor, and land that is needed to cultivate cotton and other natural fibers.

One of the most popular synthetic fabrics is called fleece, a name that originally referred to the wool from a sheep, which is still used to make fall and winter clothes. But in the twenty-first century, the word "fleece" refers to the inexpensive, lightweight, and often water-resistant synthetic material that more and more people are wearing today.

One of the most interesting things about fleece is the fact that it can be made from recycled plastic bottles. This means that fleece can be far less expensive than wool or other natural fibers. For many people, recycling plastic bottles is thought of as friendly to the natural environment since we are reusing the plastic, not burying it in the ground or dumping it in the oceans. However, in the last few years, scientists have discovered that fleece may not be as environmentally friendly as we once supposed.

Scientists are now finding very small particles of plastic at the bottom of the ocean that they believe are the remains of fleece that is washed in washing machines every day all over the world. When it is washed, more than 1,500 particles may separate from a fleece product into the water. When that water is drained, some of it will make its way back into the lakes, rivers, and oceans of our world. That is what seems to be happening now. When the synthetic particles reach natural bodies of water, the plastic is going to be eaten by fish because it looks like food to them. And sooner or later, those fish are going to be caught, delivered to the food market, and end up on your plate at dinner.

What can be done? Shall we return to more costly, heavier, and traditional natural fibers such as cotton and wool? Are people willing to spend more money to possibly save the environment? Or is economics so important to people who have very little money that they believe they cannot afford to give up their synthetic fibers?

B Read the article. Check (✓) the true statements. For statements that are false, write the true information.

1. ☐ In the developing world, 50% of people buy clothing made of synthetic fiber.

   ______

2. ☐ The word "fleece" originally meant sheep's wool.

   ______

3. ☐ Fleece is made from recycled plastic bottles.

   ______

4. ☐ More than 2,000 particles of fleece may separate during washing.

   ______

5. ☐ Fortunately, fish will not consume particles of fleece.

   ______

6. ☐ We now know that people are going to stop using fleece because of its dangers.

   ______

5 World issues

A Match the nouns and definitions.

Nouns		Definitions
1. infectious diseases	d	**a.** physical actions that are meant to cause destruction or injury
2. global warming	____	**b.** a period of time when businesses are not doing well and a large number of people cannot find jobs
3. government corruption	____	**c.** an extreme lack of money
4. famine	____	**d.** illnesses that can be passed on to other people
5. political unrest	____	**e.** a situation in which people do not have enough food
6. poverty	____	**f.** a situation in which citizens become angry or violent due to their dissatisfaction with their government
7. recession	____	**g.** illegal or dishonest activity by people with political power
8. violence	____	**h.** a situation in which a number of people are not working because they cannot find jobs
9. unemployment	____	**i.** an increase in the world's average temperatures

B Choose the correct noun from part A to complete each sentence. You will not use all of the words.

1. It seems like there are more dangerous ________________ these days, like swine flu and the Zika virus.
2. During the recent ________________, 30 percent of the businesses in my town closed, and a large part of the population didn't have jobs.
3. There's so much ________________ in this city. I'm afraid to walk on the streets alone at night because I don't feel safe.
4. Before you travel to a foreign country, make sure there are no dangerous political situations going on there. It can be unsafe to visit countries that are experiencing ________________.
5. In the 1800s, a large portion of Irish potato crops were destroyed by disease. Because potatoes were a major part of the Irish diet, there was a major ________________ and over 1.5 million people died.
6. People in this country don't trust the police or city officials because there is a lot of ________________.

6 Complete the conversations. Use the expressions in the box and the information in the list.

One thing to do . . .	The best way to fight . . .
Another thing to do . . .	One way to help . . .

- ☑ complain to the Parks Department about it
- ☐ create more government-funded jobs
- ☐ create more public housing projects
- ☐ organize a public meeting to protest the threat of public property
- ☐ educate young people about its dangers
- ☐ report it to the local newspaper
- ☐ donate money to charities that provide shelters and food

A new housing development?

1. **A:** A big housing developer wants to build an apartment complex in Forest Hill Park. I think that's terrible, but what can we do?
   B: *One thing to do is to complain to the Parks Department about it.*
   A: That's a good idea.
   B: ______________________________
2. **A:** Personally, I'm worried about violence in the city. The streets are not safe at night.
   B: ______________________________
3. **A:** You know, there's a lot of corruption in our city government.
   B: ______________________________
   A: Yeah, the bad publicity might help to clean things up a bit.
4. **A:** There are so many unemployed people in this city. I just don't know what can be done about it.
   B: ______________________________
5. **A:** What worries me most is the number of homeless people on the streets.
   B: ______________________________
   A: I agree.
   B: ______________________________

7 Complete the sentences using the present continuous passive or the present perfect passive. Then suggest a solution to each problem.

1. A lot of jobs ___have been lost___ (lose) in recent years.
   One way to deal with unemployment ___is to bring more businesses___ into the area.
2. These days, a lot of endangered animals ____________ (kill) by hunters and poachers.
   The best way to stop this practice ____________
   ____________.
3. During the past few years, lots of trees ____________ (destroy) by acid rain.
   One thing to do about it ____________
   ____________.
4. Underground water ____________ (contaminate) by agricultural pesticides.
   The best way to deal with the problem ____________
   ____________.
5. Too many people ____________ (affect) by infectious diseases in the past few years.
   The best way to stop this ____________
   ____________.

8 Write two paragraphs about a charity, an organization that helps people. In the first paragraph, describe what the charity does. In the second paragraph, explain why you think the charity is useful.

A good charity in my city is Shelter. This organization works to reduce the number of homeless people on our streets. Shelter believes the best way to do this is to . . .

Shelter is my favorite charity because homelessness is, in my opinion, the greatest problem facing my city. Many people cannot find jobs, and . . .

____
____
____
____
____
____
____
____

8 Never stop learning.

1 Choose the correct words or phrases.

1. I'm interested in human behavior, so I'm planning to take a class in ______________________. (geography / psychology / math)
2. I want to take a course in ______________________, such as commerce or accounting. (education / business / social science)
3. I'd prefer not to study ______________________ because I'm not very comfortable in hospitals. (engineering / new media / nursing)
4. I'd really like to work in Information Technology, so I'm thinking of taking courses in ______________________. (computer science / finance / English)

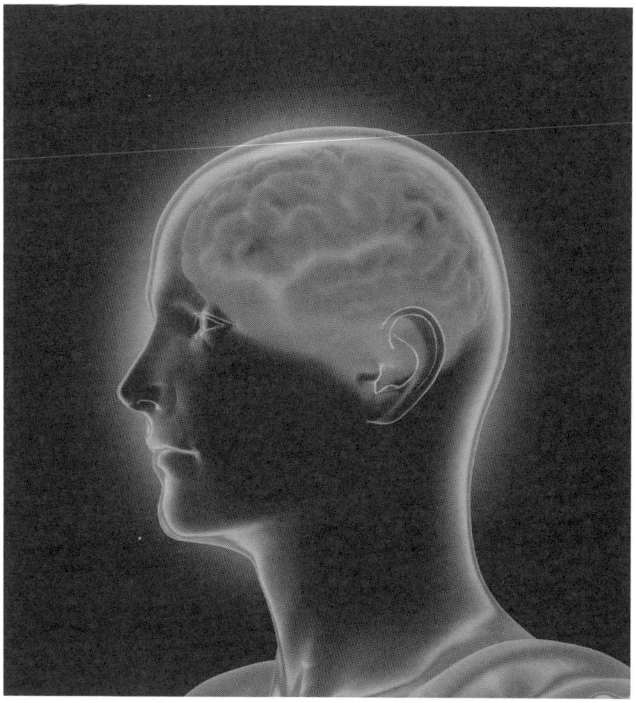

2 What would you prefer?

A Write questions with *would rather* or *would prefer* using the cues.

1. take a science class / an art class
   Would you rather take a science class or an art class? OR
   Would you prefer to take a science class or an art class?
2. study part time / full time
   ____
3. have a boring job that pays well / an exciting job that pays less
   ____
4. take a long vacation once a year / several short vacations each year
   ____

B Write answers to the questions in part A.

1. ______________________
2. ______________________
3. ______________________
4. ______________________

3 Love it or leave it

A First, complete speaker A's questions with four things you would not like to do. Use ideas in the box or your own ideas.

learn to play the accordion
learn clothing design
learn how to repair watches
study sociology
take a class in personal finance
take a cooking class

1. **A:** *Do you want to learn to play the accordion?*
   B: *I'd rather not. I'd prefer to learn to play the piano.* OR
   I'd prefer not to. I'd rather learn to play the piano.
2. **A:** Do you want to ____________________?
   B: ____________________
3. **A:** Would you like to ____________________?
   B: ____________________
4. **A:** Do you want to ____________________?
   B: ____________________
5. **A:** Would you like to ____________________?
   B: ____________________

B Now write responses for speaker B. Use the short answers *I'd rather not* or *I'd prefer not to* and say what you would prefer to do.

4 Answer these questions and give reasons.

1. On your day off, would you rather stay home or go out?
   I'd rather stay home than go out because
2. Would you prefer to have a cat or a bird?
   ____
3. Would you rather live in the city or the country?
   ____
4. When you entertain friends, would you rather invite them over for dinner or take them out to a restaurant?
   ____
5. Would you prefer to see a new movie at the theater or download it and watch it at home?
   ____

5 Online learning, the schools of the future?

A Have you taken an online class? Would you like to? Would you prefer to study online rather than at school? Write your answers.

____

____

B Read the online newspaper article. Underline the sentences that contain the answers to these questions.

1. What is a MOOC?
2. Why do so few students complete a MOOC?
3. Do professors who teach MOOCs think that they are as difficult as courses taken in a classroom?
4. What are critics of MOOCs afraid of?

FREE COLLEGE FOR EVERYONE?

posted 21st of August

A revolution in education is going to happen. Massive Online Open Courses (MOOCs for short) are designed for students who cannot afford, cannot get to, or simply don't want to attend classes in a university classroom. MOOCs are going to be of great importance to economically disadvantaged people, as well as people who live far from a university campus. The only requirement to attend a MOOC is access to a computer with an Internet connection, which is becoming more common each day.

Many MOOCs are created by top professors in their fields who teach at prestigious universities in the U.S., like Princeton, Harvard, and Stanford. These professors may teach online courses at their universities, but with a MOOC they can reach students all over the world. At the moment, not all universities accept academic credit for a MOOC. However, almost half of the professors who have taught a MOOC believe that the coursework is as demanding as the work done in a traditional university class. Many of these professors are not paid for teaching MOOCs by their universities; they do it because they want to make education available to everyone, they love teaching, and they enjoy being able to communicate with so many students online.

MOOC students do not pay tuition, which is perhaps the greatest appeal of these courses. Most professors do not even require students to buy textbooks, which can be very expensive as well. This further reduces the cost of education. On the other hand, despite the affordability of MOOCs, MOOC students do not receive diplomas, which may lessen their appeal. Students may receive certification if they pass the course, but of the 33,000 students enrolled in MOOCs today, the completion rate is strikingly low, at only 10%. Because a MOOC doesn't cost anything, students don't have to worry about losing money if they decide to drop the class. And many of them ultimately do.

So while there are upsides to MOOCs, they are not without their critics. Some professors fear that in the future there may be two kinds of university courses: expensive and superior courses at a traditional university where small groups of students meet in classes with their professors, and inexpensive and inferior massive online courses where students will never meet their professors nor even their fellow students. These critics also point out that students must be disciplined self-starters to be successful in a MOOC and that students often develop the skills of perseverance, time-management, and self-discipline by learning together with other students in a traditional university classroom.

C Write answers to these questions.

1. Do you think MOOCs are going to be the courses of the future? Why or why not?

____

____

2. What do you see as the main advantage of MOOCs? The main disadvantage?

____

____

D What would you prefer to take as a MOOC: a humanities course (such as literature, art, or history) or a science course (such as biology, chemistry, or engineering)? Why did you choose that course?

6 Complete the sentences with *by* + gerund. Use *not* if needed. Use the ideas in the box or your own information.

cook at home	eat out	go out more often	study dance
eat good food	exercise regularly	stay home	use social media

1. A good way to enjoy the weekend is *not by staying home but by going out with friends.*
2. A good way to keep in touch with old friends is ______________________
3. You can make new friends ______________________
4. The best way to save money is ______________________
5. You could stay in shape ______________________
6. I stay healthy ______________________
7. One way to learn self-confidence is ______________________

7 Choose the correct words or phrases.

1. Robin shows her ______________________ by volunteering to help people with cancer. (competitiveness / communication skills / concern for others)
2. When I was young, I didn't understand the importance of ______________________. But when I started paying my own bills, I realized it's an important skill. (money management / cooperation / perseverance)
3. I learned ______________________ from my parents. They taught me the importance of using my imagination and making art. (creativity / courtesy / self-confidence)
4. Gina always gets upset with people who disagree with her. I wish she would show more ______________________. (perseverance / self-confidence / tolerance)
5. I recently joined a choir, and I love it. But you need a lot of ______________________, because you have to practice the same piece of music for weeks before you're ready to perform it! (cooperation / perseverance / time management)

8 Personal qualities

A Read about each student in these descriptions and choose a suitable quality for each one.

☐ competitiveness	☐ creativity	☐ self-confidence	☐ time management
☐ cooperation	☐ perseverance	☐ self-discipline	☐ tolerance

1

2

4

3

1. Alex is always on time for everything. He's never even five minutes late. He keeps track of everything on his calendar. I wish I were as good at ____________ as Alex is.
2. Frank finds school very hard, but no one tries harder than he does. He always spends the whole weekend at the library trying to keep up with his studies. He shows great ____________.
3. Melissa always wants to do better than everyone else. In school, she always tries to get the best grades. Her favorite sport is field hockey because she's the best player in the school. No one needs to teach Melissa ____________.
4. Jennifer has more ____________ than any of her classmates. She writes fascinating stories that show she has a wonderful imagination. She's also very artistic and does very interesting paintings.

B Write two similar descriptions of people you know. Either use two of the qualities you didn't use in part A or choose other qualities.

1. ____

____

____

____

2. ____

____

____

____

9 My way

A List two methods of learning each of these skills.

1. become a good guitarist
   by teaching myself
   by taking lessons
2. improve my writing ability in English
   ____
   ____
3. become a more confident public speaker
   ____
   ____
4. learn more about personal finance
   ____
   ____
5. become skilled at auto repair
   ____
   ____
6. learn a new computer program
   ____
   ____

my first guitar

15 years later

B Which of the two methods in part A would you prefer to use to develop each skill? Write sentences using *would rather (not)* or *would prefer (not)*. Give reasons.

1. _I'd rather learn guitar by teaching myself than by taking lessons._
   I'd prefer not to take lessons because they're expensive.
2. ______________________
3. ______________________
4. ______________________
5. ______________________
6. ______________________

9 Getting things done

1 Which service does each person need? Choose the correct word or phrase.

- ☐ computer repair
- ☐ dry cleaning
- ☐ home repairs
- ☐ house painting
- ☐ language tutoring
- ☑ lawn mowing

1. lawn mowing
   Ken: I have a new home and don't have much time for yard work. I mowed the lawn two weeks ago, and I need to cut it again. I'd like to save money, but perhaps I'll just have to pay someone to do it for me.
2. ______________
   Akiko: I don't like the flowered wallpaper in my bedroom or the dark color of the walls in my living room. I want to have the wallpaper removed so the whole place looks bigger and brighter with fun, modern colors everywhere.
3. ______________
   Margaret: Now that it's getting colder, I need to take my winter clothes out of storage. Some things I can wash in the washing machine, but I should take my wool coat to that new place around the corner.
4. ______________
   Steven: I have a lot of work to do this week, but my laptop stopped working! I tried to fix it, but I don't know how. I can't afford to buy a new laptop.
5. ______________
   Eric: I'm so excited! I'm finally going to Quebec this summer. I studied French in high school, but I'm not sure how much I remember now. Do you know anyone who can help me improve my French?
6. ______________
   Karen: I really want to move into that studio apartment I found downtown. The only problem is that there are a lot of little things that need to be repaired. Where can I get a leaky faucet and a broken lock repaired?

home repairs

language tutoring

lawn mowing

2 Where can I get . . . ?

A Match the verbs in column A with the nouns in column B.

A	B	
cut	a stain	**1.** cut my hair
check	my blood pressure	**2.**
do	my computer	**3.**
fix	my hair	**4.**
print	my nails	**5.**
remove	my pants	**6.**
shorten	my photos	**7.**

B First, use the items in part A to write *Where can I get . . . ?* or *Where can I have . . . ?* questions for speaker A. Then write responses for speaker B using your own ideas.

1. **A:** Where can I get my hair cut?
   B: You can get it cut at May's Salon.
2. **A:** ______
   B: ______
3. **A:** ______
   B: ______
4. **A:** ______
   B: ______
5. **A:** ______
   B: ______
6. **A:** ______
   B: ______
7. **A:** ______
   B: ______

3 Where can you have these services done? Write sentences with *You can have . . . .*

Come to
SALON 21
for an
AMAZING
haircut!

1. You can have your hair cut at Salon 21.
____

At ***KWIK FIX***
we repair all kinds
of shoes.

2. ______________________________
____

DREAM CLEAN
We dry-clean
your clothes
like no
one else.

3. ______________________________
____

CARPET WORLD
We'll clean your carpets so they're as good as new.

4. ______________________________
____

We do nails (and only nails)
at **Nail File.**

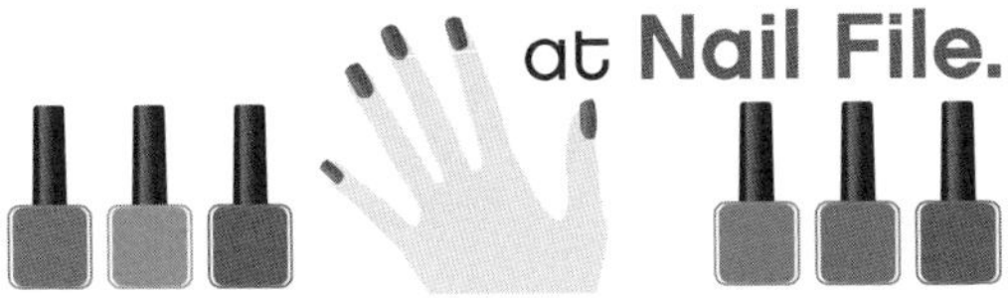

5. ______________________________
____

JIMMY'S...

...the best car wash in town!

6. ______________________________
____

Service your washing machine to keep it running its best.

Call Hal's Repairs at 555-1838

7. ______________________________
____

At EYE to EYE,

we can examine your eyes
in 30 minutes.

8. ______________________________
____

4 Less could be better

A Look at the two pictures. Where have you dreamed about living, in an apartment in the city or in a house in the suburbs? Why? Where would your parents like to live? Why?

DOWNSIZING

Do you want your parents' furniture, family photos, old toys, and sports equipment? If you're a millennial, the answer is likely to be "no."

Millennials are people who became adults at the beginning of the 21st century, and they are not necessarily interested in collecting things. And boomers, Americans born in the years after World War II, are finding out that their children have very different ideas about how to live "the good life."

Millennials do not feel the need to have a lot of *things*. They would rather have *experiences*, like tourism, art, and sports activities. This preference for "less is better" – or downsizing – is partly a result of the world economic crisis and the student debt that many young adults have. The lack of jobs has made millennials want to lower their expenses. And they feel that they must pay off their student loans before they can get married and have children of their own.

Because millennials are waiting to start families, they tend to prefer to live in apartments rather than large houses like their parents. First, they simply don't need that much space. Second, houses are expensive. Third, houses are often located in the suburbs, farther away from the culture and diversity that cities have to offer and that many millennials want.

But, in the latest twist of generational clashes, millennials are finding it more and more difficult to afford city living. Boomers, who generally have more money to spend than millennials, are finally ready to sell their houses now that their children have moved out. When they do, many then use that money to buy an apartment in the city where they can start a new life with all the amenities cities have to offer to people with money.

With this increase in demand, the prices of apartments have gone up, and millennials are discovering that it is very difficult to compete economically with their boomer parents. One option is for millennials to live together. Today some of them are renting houses or large apartments that several people can share. More than a few people think that this kind of downsizing, besides being good for the pocketbook, is good for the planet.

B Read the article about downsizing. Check (✓) the true statements. For statements that are false, write the true information.

1. ☐ Adult children still enjoy receiving furniture from their parents.

___

2. ☐ Boomers are Americans born before World War II.

___

3. ☐ Downsizing is the philosophy that "less is better."

___

4. ☐ The competition between boomers and millennials has a lot to do with money.

___

5. ☐ The next step in downsizing could be for boomers and millennials to share houses and large apartments.

___

5 Write two suggestions for each of these problems.

1. **A:** I never have any energy, so I can never do anything except work. I sleep all weekend, so don't tell me to get more rest!

   B: Have you thought about taking an aerobics class?
   Another option is to improve your diet.

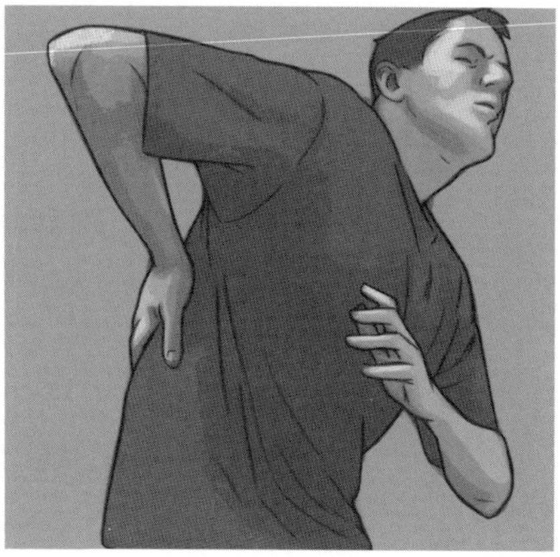

2. **A:** My problem is a constant backache. I just don't know what to do to get rid of it. I had someone give me a massage, but it didn't really help.

   B: Maybe you could ______________________
   ____

3. **A:** My doctor told me to get more exercise. She strongly recommended swimming, but I find swimming so boring! In fact, aren't all sports boring?

   B: Why don't you ______________________
   ____

4. **A:** I'm very sociable, and I have great difficulty saying no. I end up doing things every night of the week – going to parties, clubs, the movies. I'm so tired all the time!

   B: It might be a good idea ______________________
   ____

5. **A:** I like to be a good neighbor, but the woman next door drives me crazy. She's always knocking on my door to chat. And whenever I go out into the yard, she goes into her yard – and talks for hours!

   B: What about ______________________
   ____

6 Choose the correct three-word phrasal verb for each sentence.

1. I don't know how my grandmother ______________________ all the new technology. She's better at understanding new gadgets than I am! (comes up with / cuts down on / keeps up with)
2. My cousin didn't know what to do for her mother's 60th birthday, but she finally ______________________ the idea of a surprise picnic with the whole family. (came up with / got along with / looked forward to)
3. Ilene has done it again! She only met Chris two months ago, and already she has ______________________ him. Why doesn't she try to work out any problems? (broken up with / gotten along with / kept up with)
4. After Michelle saw her doctor, she decided to ______________________ eating fast food. She wants to lose some weight and start exercising again in order to keep fit. (cut down on / look forward to / take care of)
5. We're really lucky in my family because we all ______________________ each other very well. (come up with / get along with / look forward to)
6. I've done pretty badly in my classes this semester, so I'm not really ______________________ receiving my grades. (getting along with / looking forward to / taking care of)
7. I can't ______________________ that loud music anymore! I can't stand hip-hop, and I'm going to tell my neighbor right now. (cut down on / put up with / take care of)
8. I've been getting sick a lot lately, and I often feel tired. I really need to start ______________________ my health. (cutting down on / keeping up with / taking care of)

10 A matter of time

1 Circle the correct word that describes each sentence.

1. Events in December 2010 led to the peaceful removal of Tunisia's prime minister in January 2011. (natural disaster / epidemic / revolution)
2. In 2014, a new species of insect was found in Vietnam. It has a body over 30 centimeters long and is the second longest insect in the world. (discovery / invention / epidemic)
3. On June 12, 2016, a gunman entered a nightclub in Florida where he killed 49 people and injured more than 50. (invention / terrorist act / achievement)
4. Advances in robot technology have come a long way in recent years. Scientists like Japan's Hiroshi Ishiguro have created human-like robots that can have conversations with each other and with humans. (achievement / disaster / terrorist act)
5. Prime Minister Benazir Bhutto of Pakistan was killed after leaving a campaign rally in December 2007. (assassination / election / revolution)
6. In 2010, a series of floods in Australia affected over 200,000 people and caused nearly a billion Australian dollars in damage. (discovery / natural disaster / epidemic)

2 Complete the sentences. Use words from the box.

ago	for	from	in	since	to

1. Jazz first became popular ___in___ the 1920s.
2. The cell phone was invented about 45 years ________.
3. Brasília has been the capital city of Brazil ________ 1960.
4. The first laptop was produced ________ 1981.
5. Mexico has been independent ________ more than 200 years.
6. World War II lasted ________ 1939 ________ 1945.
7. Vietnam was separated into two parts ________ about 20 years.
8. East and West Germany have been united ________ 1990.

jazz

Brasília

3 Nouns and verbs

A Complete this chart. Then check your answers in a dictionary.

Noun	Verb	Noun	Verb
achievement	achieve	existence	
assassination		exploration	
demonstration		explosion	
discovery		invention	
discrimination		transformation	
election		vaccination	

B Choose verbs from the chart in part A to complete these sentences. Use the correct verb tense.

Bangalore, a high-tech center

a research station in Antarctica

1. Over the past several decades, the Indian city of Bangalore has transformed itself into a high-tech center.
2. In World War I, many soldiers were ______________ against typhoid, a deadly bacterial disease.
3. Aung San, the man who led Myanmar to independence, was ______________ in 1947. No one is certain who killed him.
4. The European Union has ______________ since 1957.
5. Until the 1960s, there were many laws that ______________ against African Americans in certain regions of the United States.
6. In 1885, Louis Pasteur ______________ a cure for rabies when he treated a young boy who was bitten by a dog.
7. In recent years, teams of experts in countries such as Cambodia and Angola have been safely ______________ land mines in order to rid those countries of these dangerous weapons.
8. One of the few parts of the world that has not been ______________ much is Antarctica. The extreme climate makes it dangerous to travel far from research centers.

4 Vaccines past, present, and future

A What are vaccinations? If necessary, scan the article to find out.

VACCINATIONS

For well over a thousand years, smallpox was a disease that everyone feared. The disease killed much of the native population in South America when the Spanish arrived there in the early sixteenth century. By the end of the eighteenth century, smallpox was responsible for the deaths of about one in ten people around the world. Those who survived the disease were left with ugly scars on their skin.

It had long been well known among farmers that people who worked with cows rarely caught smallpox; instead, they often caught a similar but much milder disease called cowpox. A British doctor named Edward Jenner was fascinated by this, and so he studied cowpox. He became convinced that, by injecting people with cowpox, he could protect them against the much worse disease smallpox. In 1796, he vaccinated a boy with cowpox and, two months later, with smallpox. The boy did not get smallpox. In the next two years, Jenner vaccinated several children in the same way, and none of them got the disease.

News of Jenner's success soon spread. In 1800, the Royal Vaccine Institution was founded in Berlin, Germany. In the following year, Napoleon opened a similar institute in Paris, France. It took nearly two centuries to achieve Jenner's dream of ridding the world of smallpox. In 1967, the World Health Organization (WHO) started an ambitious vaccination program, and the last known case of smallpox was recorded in Somalia in 1977.

The future of vaccinations aims at the eradication of three diseases that can be caused by mosquito bites: malaria, Zika virus, and dengue. Malaria is an infectious disease that is still a problem, in part because the virus that causes the disease hides in the cells away from the immune system. Zika virus has recently been discovered in various places all over the world, and it is particularly dangerous for pregnant women. At this time there is no vaccine for Zika virus, although scientists are working on one. Dengue is a disease that has multiplied alarmingly in recent years, but in the last two years a vaccine has been successfully developed for people between 9 and 45 years old.

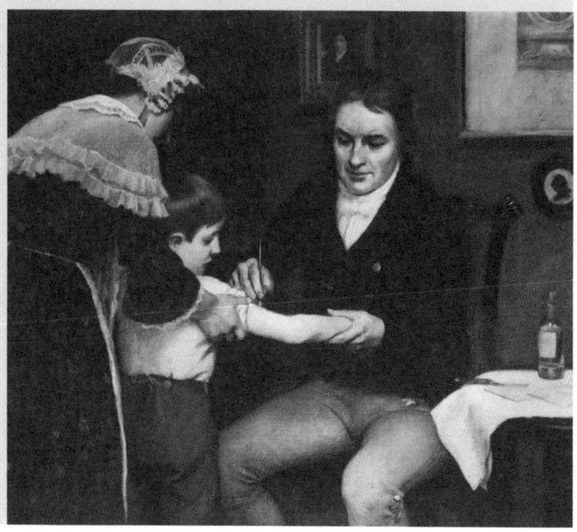

B Read the article about vaccinations. Complete the chart with the history of events in the story of vaccinations.

Date	Event
1. Early 16th century	*Smallpox killed much of the native population in South America.*
2. End of the 18th century	
3. 1796	
4. 1800	
5. 1801	
6. 1967	
7. 1977	
8. Future challenge	

5 Life in 2050

A Complete these predictions about life in 2050. Use the future continuous of the verb given. Then add two more predictions of your own.

Life on the moon?

By 2050, . . .

1. some people ______will be living______ in cities on the moon. (live)
2. many people ____________ temperature-controlled body suits. (wear)
3. most people ____________ cars that run on fuel from garbage. (drive)
4. people ____________ in a new Olympic event – mind reading. (compete)
5. ____________
6. ____________

B Complete these predictions about what will have happened by 2050. Use the future perfect. Then add two more predictions of your own.

By 2050, . . .

1. computers ______will have replaced______ people as translators. (replace)
2. ties for men ____________ out of fashion. (go)
3. scientists ____________ a cheap way of getting drinking water from seawater. (discover)
4. medical researchers ____________ a cure for cancer. (find)
5. ____________
6. ____________

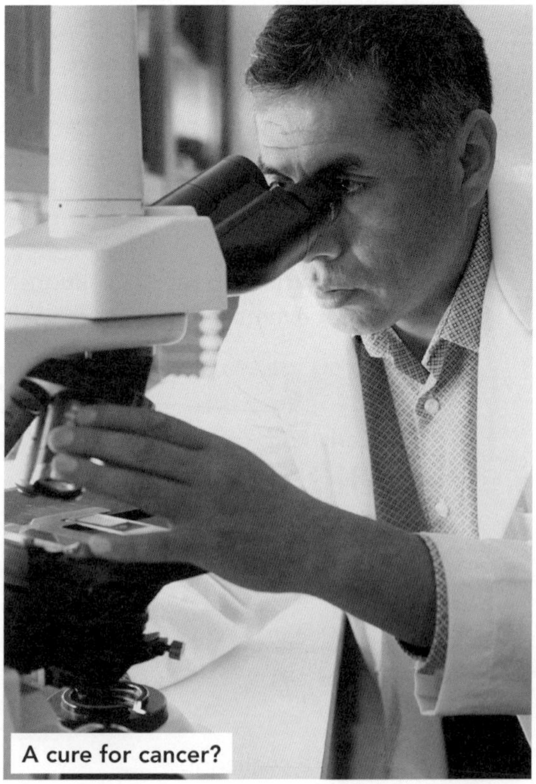

A cure for cancer?

6 Write two responses to each question.

1. What will or won't you be doing in ten years? (Use the future continuous.)

   I won't be living with my parents.

2. How will cities of the future be different? (Use *will*.)

   Cities won't allow cars downtown.

3. How will life in small villages in your country have changed in the next 20 years? (Use the future perfect.)

   More people will have moved back from cities to small villages.

4. How do you think the world's weather will change during this century? (Use *will*.)

   The weather will be warmer, and the summers will be longer.

5. What advances will scientists have made by 2050? (Use the future perfect.)

   Scientists will have found a way to grow enough food for everyone.

7 Think of four more ways that technology will affect how we live and work in the next 20 years.

1. Robots will be cleaning our homes.
2. ______________________________
3. ______________________________
4. ______________________________
5. ______________________________

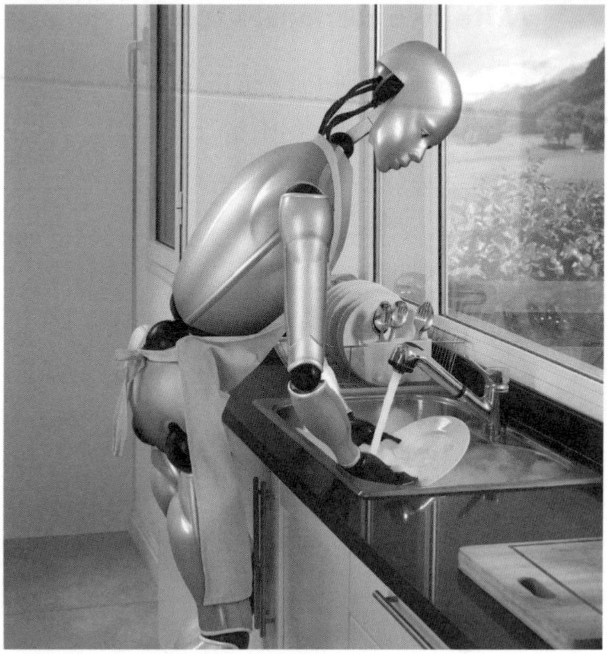

8 Write two paragraphs about one of these topics or a topic of your choice. In the first paragraph, describe the past. In the second paragraph, describe how you think the future will be.

a music group	changes within a country	health
space exploration	changes within a region	technology

Eyeglasses were invented in the 13th century in Italy. These early glasses didn't include earpieces to keep the glasses on the wearer's face. Instead, they had to be held in front of the eyes or placed on the nose. In the 1700s, eyeglasses were designed with earpieces, making them easier to use. In the 20th century, contacts became common, making it even easier and more convenient for people to use corrective lenses.

Technological advances have continued to make vision correction more practical and convenient. In recent years, doctors have developed laser surgery techniques, which can make corrective lenses unnecessary for people with certain types of vision problems. In the future, computer technology will probably replace eyeglasses, contact lenses, and laser surgery. It may even make it possible for blind people to see.

11 Rites of passage

1 Milestones

A Read these statements. Check (✓) the ones that are true for you. For statements that are false, write the true information.

Example: As soon as I got my first cell phone, I called all my friends.

The moment I got a cell phone, I called my parents OR *I've never had a cell phone.*

1. ☐ By the time I was three years old, I had already learned two languages.
2. ☐ Before I started school, I was carefree – I used to watch TV all day.
3. ☐ After I started taking the bus by myself, I became more independent.
4. ☐ As soon as I got my driver's license, my parents let me drive everywhere.
5. ☐ The moment I earned my own money, I opened a bank account.
6. ☐ Once I started learning English, I quit studying other languages.
7. ☐ Until I graduated from high school, I was very unsophisticated.
8. ☐ Before I became more independent, I thought I knew more than my parents.

B Write three true statements about how things have changed over time for you, your family, or your friends. Use time clauses.

1. ______________________________
2. ______________________________
3. ______________________________

2 Complete these descriptions. Use words from the box.

☐ ambitious	☐ carefree	☐ rebellious
☐ argumentative	☐ naive	☑ sophisticated

1. Sandra is so ___sophisticated___. She always dresses well, she knows lots of intelligent people, and she never says anything silly.
2. I just spent a horrible evening with Patricia. She questioned and criticized everything I said. I wish she weren't so ________________.
3. My sister is very ________________. She trusts everyone and thinks everyone is good.
4. Once I turned 16, I became less ________________, and my parents started to let me do what I wanted.
5. Eric is really ________________. He wants to own his own business by the time he's 25.
6. I wish I could be like Susie. She's so ________________ and never seems to worry about anything.

3 Do you have a friend who is special to you? Write about him or her. In the first paragraph, describe the person. In the second paragraph, describe a particular time when the person helped you.

One of my best friends is Jennifer. She's very mature and conscientious, and she always gives me good advice. Until I met her, I had been making some bad decisions . . . .

Jennifer is also very generous. She always helps her friends when they need it. For example, the moment she found out I was sick last winter, she came over and visited me.

____

____

____

____

____

____

____

____

4 Turning points

A Scan the article from a sports magazine about Usain Bolt. What lesson did he learn as a child?

LEARNING FAST

Usain Bolt is called "Lightning" Bolt because he is considered the fastest man in the world. The Jamaican runner is an Olympic champion in the 100- and 200-meter **sprint**, as well as in the 4x100 relay, a race in which four runners each sprint 100 meters and then pass the baton to the next runner. He is the first man in the modern Olympic Games to win nine gold medals in the sprint. He is also the first athlete to win gold medals in the 100- and 200-meter races as well as in the 4x100 relay race in three Olympic Games, in 2008, 2012, and 2016.

In his autobiography, *Faster than Lightning*, Bolt writes that sports interested him most as a child. He also says that in school he learned something important about himself: he is ambitious because he loves to compete and to win.

He doesn't want to be one of the **runners-up**. This desire to be the best, plus his natural physical speed, brought him to the attention of Pablo McNeil, the former Olympic sprinter who was teaching athletics at Bolt's high school. Pablo McNeil convinced him to concentrate on sprinting and trained him in that sport.

When he was 15, Bolt **launched himself into** world-class athletics in the 2002 World Junior Championships in Jamaica's capital, Kingston. He was so nervous that he put his shoes on the wrong feet! But that was another important lesson: he would never allow stress to affect him again before a race. In spite of his nervousness, he became the youngest World Junior athlete to win the **prestigious** gold medal when he ran in the 200-meter sprint.

At the 2008 Olympic Games, Bolt learned another lesson: he should never stop learning. He broke two records at those games, becoming the fastest sprinter in the 100- and 200-meter race. At the end of the 100-meter race, he shocked everyone when he slowed down before the finish line. He was **ecstatic** because he already knew he was the winner. Some people felt he was too carefree. They thought he should have sprinted all the way. In the following 200-meter race, he didn't slow down. He ran all the way in **record time**, like the fastest man in the world.

B Read the article. Look at the words and phrases in bold in the article. Write definitions or synonyms for each word or phrase.

1. sprint ______________________
2. runners-up ______________________
3. launched himself into ______________________
4. prestigious ______________________
5. ecstatic ______________________
6. record time ______________________

C What factors mentioned in the article do you think have helped Usain Bolt to become a successful athlete?

____

5 Write sentences about your regrets. Use *should (not) have.*

1. I spent all my money on clothes. Now I can't afford to take a vacation.
   I shouldn't have spent all my money on clothes.
2. I was very argumentative with my boss, so she fired me.
3. I changed jobs. Now I work in a bank. My job isn't very interesting.
4. I bought a new TV with my credit card. Now I can't afford the payments.
5. I studied music in school, but I'm much better at computer science.
6. I was completely rebellious when I was a student, so I got very bad grades.
7. My friend asked to copy my homework, so I let him. The teacher found out and gave us both Fs.
8. My cousin invited me to a party. I accepted but didn't put the date in my calendar. I forgot all about it.
9. I was very naive when I was younger. I lent money to people, but they hardly ever paid me back.
10. My friend asked for my opinion on her new hairstyle. I told her I didn't like it. Now she's not talking to me.

6 *If . . .*

A Rewrite the sentences as hypothetical situations. Use the words given.

1. I should have studied English sooner. (get a better job)
   If I'd studied English sooner, I would have gotten a better job.
2. We should have made a reservation. (eat already)
   ____
3. I should have put on sunscreen. (not get a sunburn)
   ____
4. You should have let me drive. (arrive by now)
   ____
5. I should have ignored your text in class. (not get in trouble)
   ____

B Write sentences describing hypothetical situations. Use the words given and your own ideas.

1. dependable *If I had been more dependable as a teenager, my parents would have let me borrow the car more often.*
2. ambitious ______________________________
3. pragmatic ______________________________
4. naive ______________________________
5. rebellious ______________________________
6. wise ______________________________

7 Complete the conversation. Circle the correct time expressions and use the correct tense of the verbs given.

Hector: I've made such a mess of my life!

Scott: What do you mean?

Hector: If I ___hadn't accepted___ (not accept) a job (as soon as / before / until) I graduated, I ______________ (travel) around South America all summer – just like you did. You were so carefree.

Scott: You know, I should ______________ (not go) to South America. I should ______________ (take) the great job I was offered. (After / Before / Until) I returned from South America, it was too late.

Hector: But my job is so depressing! (Before / The moment / Until) I started it, I hated it – on the very first day! That was five years ago, and nothing's changed. I should ______________ (look) for another job right away.

Scott: Well, start looking now. I posted my résumé online last month, and five companies contacted me right away. If I ______________ (not post) my résumé, no one ______________ (contact) me. I accepted one of the job offers.

Hector: Really? What's the job?

Scott: It's working as a landscape gardener. (Before / The moment / Until) I saw it, I knew it was right for me.

Hector: But for me right now, the problem is that I get a very good salary and I just bought a house. If I ______________ (not buy) the house, I ______________ (be able to) take a lower paying job.

Scott: Well, I guess you can't have everything. If I ______________ (have) a better salary, I ______________ (buy) a house, too.

12 Keys to success

1 Complete these sentences with *In order for* or *In order to.*

1. In order for ______ a restaurant to be popular, it has to have attractive decor.
2. ______ a movie to be entertaining, it has to have good actors and an interesting story.
3. ______ succeed in business, you often have to work long hours.
4. ______ attract new members, a sports club needs to offer inexpensive memberships.
5. ______ speak a foreign language well, it's a good idea to use the language as often as possible.
6. ______ a clothing store to succeed, it has to be able to find the latest fashions.

2 Write sentences. Use the information in the box.

☐ have talented salespeople	☐ work extremely long hours
☑ keep up with your studies	☐ provide excellent customer service
☐ be clever and entertaining	☐ have drama and interesting characters

1. be a successful student
   In order to be a successful student, you have to keep up with your studies.
2. a clothes store to be profitable
   For a clothes store to be profitable, ______
3. manage your own business
   ______
4. an advertisement to be persuasive
   ______
5. run a successful automobile company
   ______
6. a reality TV show to be successful
   ______

3 Choose the correct word or phrase.

1. I didn't enjoy this book on how to succeed in business. It wasn't very ___well written___. (affordable / well paid / well written)
2. I learned a lot about how to run a successful bookstore from taking that class. I found it very ________________. (attractive / informative / knowledgeable)
3. Annie has so many interesting ideas, and she's always thinking of new projects. She's very ________________. (clever / entertaining / tough)
4. Debra is a salesperson, and she's good at her job. She's so ________________ that she sells three times as much as her co-workers. (unfriendly / affordable / persuasive)
5. Matthew is one of the top models in Milan. He goes to the gym every day, so he looks really ________________. (clever / charming / muscular)
6. Before opening a new store, it's important to think through all of your ideas and have ________________. (competitive salaries / a clear business plan / a reliable job)
7. My new job has great benefits. We have unlimited time off, excellent health insurance, and ________________. (a good product / flexible working hours / a crowdfunding platform)

4 Read this information about journalists. Then write a paragraph about one of the people in the box or another person of your choice.

To be a successful journalist, you need to be both talented and dynamic. You have to write well and write quickly. In order to report the news, a journalist needs to have a good knowledge of world and current events. In addition, you must be able to report a story accurately.

an artist | a boss | a homemaker | a parent | a teacher

5 I like it because . . .

A For each pair of pictures, write one sentence about what you like and one sentence about what you dislike. Give reasons using the words given.

1. I like this park because it's clean and there are a lot of trees. (because)

I don't like this park since ______________________ (since)

2. ______________________ (since)

______________________ (the reason)

3. ______________________ (because of)

______________________ (due to)

B Think of an example in your city of each of these places: a restaurant, a hotel, and a shopping center. Write a sentence about why you like or dislike each one.

Example: The reason I don't like Cho Dang Gol Restaurant in my hometown is its noisy location right by the freeway.

1. ______________________

2. ______________________

3. ______________________

6 A new business with an ancient product

A Scan the article about Andean Grain. What is the secret that the company is selling?

SELLING SECRETS OF THE PAST

The Argentinian company Andean Grain is contributing to a **comeback** of highly nutritious foods that were unknown to many people during the last few hundred years. Andean Grain sells foods made from **indigenous** Latin American plants, like chia seeds, amaranth, and quinoa. These plants are coming **to prominence** today because knowledgeable people have discovered that chia seeds, amaranth, and quinoa are **superfoods**, incredibly rich in vitamins and proteins.

Chia seeds were grown by the Aztecs as an energy food. In order to travel long distances without having to stop, they drank a beverage consisting of chia seeds, lemon juice, and water. The Aztecs also cultivated amaranth, which they believed was a superfood, as do scientists today. Quinoa was grown in the mountains of the Andes by the Incas. All three of these foods **went out of favor** after the conquest of Latin America in the 16th century. Wheat was preferred over these native plants, and they were almost unknown outside the countries that grew them. Nevertheless, these foods have become popular once more due to the health benefits that they are supposed to provide.

They appear to be of optimal benefit for the heart and brain, and **rumor has it** that they may help prevent cancer. They're also gluten-free. Because many people today have problems digesting the gluten in wheat, gluten-free foods have become very fashionable.

As a result, there is a great demand by the public for these superfoods. Andean Grain sells its products all over the world, but it is especially active in Europe, where it has a main office in the United Kingdom. From its base in Argentina, Andean Grain sends most of its native plants to Europe to be made into affordable breads, breakfast cereals, and today's popular trail mixes, which are combinations of dried fruits, nuts, and seeds.

The secret is out, and what was hidden from the world for so many centuries has today become an important discovery of foods for our health. Did you know about these superfoods before the rest of the world discovered them just a few years ago?

B Read the article. Look at the words and phrases in bold in the article. Write definitions or synonyms for each word or phrase.

1. comeback ______
2. indigenous ______
3. to prominence ______
4. superfood ______
5. went out of favor ______
6. rumor has it ______

7 Look at these advertisements and write two sentences about each one. Describe the features and give reasons why you like or dislike the advertisements.

Example: I like the first ad because it attracts your attention.

I like the second ad because it has a simple and clean design.

1. ____

____

____

____

2. ____

____

____

____

8 Do you have the right qualities?

A Complete the sentences with the words from the box.

affordable	**athletic**	**clever**	**entertaining**	**informative**	**knowledgeable**	**muscular**	**salesperson**

1. I'm not ______________ enough about tools to be a successful salesperson in a hardware store. I'm familiar with some common tools, but I don't know how to use most tools.
2. To be successful, personal trainers need to be fit and ______________.
3. *Weekend Talk* ran for only three months because it was so boring. For a TV show to be successful on Saturday evenings, it really has to be ______________.
4. I wouldn't be a good ______________ because I'm not very persuasive.
5. I found a fantastic news website this morning. It's really ______________. It has very detailed stories about local and international news.
6. For a salesperson to be persuasive, he or she has to be ______________ with words.
7. Kate is so ______________. She plays soccer, tennis, and basketball, and she's excellent at all three sports.
8. I like this store, but it's not very ______________. Even the small items are expensive.

B Write sentences using the words below and infinitive clauses with *to* or *for*.

1. apply for a job / write a good résumé

   ____

2. be an effective personal trainer / listen to your clients' needs

   ____

3. a restaurant / be successful / delicious food at good prices

   ____

4. students / get good grades / study hard and do their best

   ____

5. learn a new language / practice every day

   ____

13 What might have been

1 What do you think happened? Write an explanation for each event using past modals.

1. She may have lost her car key.

2.

3.

4.

5.

6.

2 Write two paragraphs about something strange that has happened to you. In the first paragraph, describe the situation. In the second paragraph, give two or three explanations for what happened.

I invited six friends to a barbecue on the beach. I suggested we meet at eight o'clock. They all said they would come and bring some food.

On the day of the barbecue, only two of my friends showed up. I guess my other friends could have overslept, or they might have decided to do something else. Another possibility is that they may have thought I meant 8 P.M. instead of 8 A.M. I'm not sure what happened!

____

____

____

____

____

____

____

____

3 Answer these questions. Write two explanations using past modals.

Why do you think the ancient Britons built Stonehenge?

1. They might have built it to use as a church.

2. ____

How do you think early explorers communicated with people in the places they visited?

3. They could have ____

4. ____

How do you think the early Polynesians were able to travel across vast oceans?

5. They may have ____

6. ____

4 Strange creatures

A Skim the online article about a world-famous legend. Where does the legend come from?

HOME NEWS SPOTLIGHT LOCATIONS COMMUNITY

BIGFOOT

He has been described as a gigantic, hairy, mysterious man-like creature that lives in the forests of the Pacific Northwest of the U.S. and avoids people. He is called Bigfoot because of the big footprints people have found in the earth.

Scientists who seriously consider the possibility of Bigfoot's existence offer the explanation of ancient man-like apes that might have survived in small groups. The most popular possibility is Gigantopithecus, an ape that lived until about 100,000 years ago, was three meters (9.8 feet) tall, and weighed more than 500 kilos (1,102 pounds). Unfortunately, there are two problems with this possibility. Most scientists believe that Gigantopithecus would have walked on its hands and legs because its weight would have been too much for its legs and ankles to support. Also, the bones of this ape have only been found in Asia. It's more likely that people saw a large black bear that walks on its two legs, common in the Pacific Northwest, and they thought it was Bigfoot.

Another explanation for this mystery is that it's a hoax, a false story that some people invent as a joke. And of course they can make money by selling their story to television shows and newspapers. There have been quite a few hoaxes in the last few years. Some were very convincing, but all were proved false. If it seems quite certain that Bigfoot couldn't have existed, why do people continue to believe in creatures like this? British anthropologist Jane Goodall may have come up with the best explanation: "Well, I'm a romantic, so I always wanted them to exist."

B Read the article. Then write answers to the questions.

1. How might someone describe Bigfoot?

   ____

2. Imagine that you have seen a creature resembling Bigfoot. Do you think you would have believed it was Bigfoot? Why or why not?

   ____

3. What is the most popular possible explanation for Bigfoot from scientists?

   ____

4. What is one problem with this popular explanation?

   ____

5. What do you think people might have seen when they thought they saw Bigfoot?

   ____

5 Should have, could have, would have

A What should or shouldn't these people have done? Read each situation and check (✓) the best suggestion.

1. Mrs. King wouldn't let her children watch TV for a month because they broke a window playing baseball.
   - ☐ She could have made them pay for the window.
   - ☐ She shouldn't have done anything. It was an accident.
   - ☐ She shouldn't have let them play baseball for a month.
2. Steve's old car broke down on the highway late one night, and his cell phone battery was dead. He left the car on the side of the road and walked home.
   - ☐ He should have stopped a stranger's car to ask for a ride.
   - ☐ He could have slept in his car till morning.
   - ☐ He should have walked to the nearest pay phone and called a tow truck.
3. Sarah was in a park. She saw some people leave all their trash after they had finished their picnic. She did nothing.
   - ☐ She did the right thing.
   - ☐ She should have asked them to throw away their trash.
   - ☐ She could have thrown away the trash herself.
4. Edward's neighbors were renovating their kitchen. They made a lot of noise every day until midnight. Edward called the police.
   - ☐ He shouldn't have called the police.
   - ☐ He should have realized that they were trying to finish the job quickly.
   - ☐ He could have asked them not to make any noise in the evenings.
5. Barbara's boss borrowed $20 from her a month ago, but he forgot to pay her back. Barbara never said anything about it.
   - ☐ She should have demanded her money back.
   - ☐ She shouldn't have loaned it to him.
   - ☐ She could have written him a nice email asking for the money.

B What would you have done in the situations in part A? Write suggestions or comments using past modals.

1. I would have made them pay for the window.
2. ______________________
3. ______________________
4. ______________________
5. ______________________

6 Nouns and verbs

A Complete the chart.

Noun	Verb	Noun	Verb
assumption	assume	___________	predict
criticism	___________	suggestion	___________
demand	___________	suspect	___________
excuse	___________	warning	___________

B Complete the sentences using words from the chart in part A. For the verbs, use *shouldn't have* + past participle. For the nouns, use the appropriate singular or plural form.

1. Last year some economists said that food and gas prices wouldn't increase. Those ____predictions____ were wrong! Both food and gas are more expensive now.
2. Christopher ______________________ having a beach party. It was so dark, I stepped in a hole and hurt my ankle.
3. Andy bought an expensive ring and gave it to Millie for her birthday. A year later, he asked her to marry him. When she said no, he made an outrageous ______________________. He said he wanted his ring back!
4. I ______________________ my co-worker not to be late for work so often. It was really none of my business.
5. Lori said she was late because she got caught in traffic. Hmm. I've heard that ______________________ before.
6. Kevin ______________________ I would still be awake at midnight. I was asleep when he called.
7. I thought that my roommate had taken my wallet, but I found it at the bottom of my bag. I ______________________ that my roommate took it. He would never do something like that.
8. James ______________________ me for wearing jeans and a T-shirt to a friend's party. He always has negative things to say.

7 Complete these conversations. Use the past modals in the box and the verbs given. (More than one modal is possible.)

could have	may have	might have	must have	should have

1. **A:** Where's Luke? He's late.
   B: He ___may have gotten___ (get) stuck in rush-hour traffic.
   A: He's always late! You know, he ___should have taken___ (take) the subway.
2. **A:** Judy never responded to my invitation.
   B: She ______________ (not receive) it. You ______________ (call) her.
3. **A:** Matt hasn't answered his phone for a week.
   B: He ______________ (go) on vacation. He ______________ (tell) you, though – sometimes he's very inconsiderate.
4. **A:** I can never get in touch with Kathy. She never returns phone calls or answers texts!
   B: Yeah, I have the same problem with her. Her voice mail ______________ (run out) of space. She ______________ (get) a new phone service by now.
5. **A:** Thomas is strange. Sometimes he works really hard, but sometimes he seems pretty lazy. Last week, he hardly did any work.
   B: Well, you know, he ______________ (not feel) well. Still, he ______________ (tell) you that he was sick.
6. **A:** I ordered a book online a month ago, but it still hasn't arrived.
   B: They ______________ (have) a problem with the warehouse, but they ______________ (let) you know.

14 Creative careers

1 Complete the conversation. Use the passive form of the verbs given.

Anna: Putting on a fashion show must be really fun!

Marcus: Yeah, but it's also challenging. All the clothes have to ___be numbered___ (number) so that the models wear them in the right sequence. And they also have to ______________ (mark) with the name of the right model.

Anna: What happens if something ______________ (wear) by the wrong model?

Marcus: Well, if it doesn't fit, it looks terrible! First impressions are very important. A lot of clothes ______________ (sell) because they look good at the show.

Anna: Do you have to rehearse for a fashion show?

Marcus: Of course! There's more involved than just models and clothes. Special lighting ______________ (use), and music ______________ (play) during the show.

Anna: It sounds complicated.

Marcus: Oh, it is. And at some fashion shows, a commentary may ______________ (give).

Anna: A commentary? What do you mean?

Marcus: Well, someone talks about the clothes as they ______________ (show) on the runway by the models.

Anna: It sounds like timing is really important.

Marcus: Exactly. Everything has to ______________ (time) perfectly! Otherwise, the show may ______________ (ruin).

2 Choose the correct words or phrases.

1. Often, special music has to be ______________________ for a film.
(written / designed / hired)

2. A play may be ______________________ for several weeks before it is shown to the public.
(shot / taken / rehearsed)

3. Designing ______________________ for actors to wear requires a lot of creativity.
(scripts / movies / clothes)

4. Newspapers are ______________________ to stores after they are printed.
(written / delivered / reported)

5. ______________________ are added after the film has been put together.
(Scenes / Sound effects / Actors)

3 Complete this passage. Use the passive form of the verbs given.

1. Nowadays, all sorts of things ___*are produced*___ (produce) in factories, including lettuce! At one food factory, fresh green lettuce ______________________ (grow) without sunlight or soil. Here is how it ______________________ (do).
2. Lettuce seedlings ______________________ (place) at one end of a long production line. Conveyor belts ______________________ (use) to move the seedlings slowly along. The tiny plants ______________________ (expose) to light from fluorescent lamps.
3. They have to ______________________ (feed) through the roots with plant food and water that ______________________ (control) by a computer.
4. Thirty days later, the plants ______________________ (collect) at the other end of the conveyor belts.
5. They may ______________________ (deliver) to the vegetable market the same day.

4 Professional fashion blogger

A Scan the article and use the past participle form of the words in the box to complete the sentences with the passive voice.

concern	**create**	**inspire**	**interest**	**interview**	**notice**

A Passion for Fashion

In just the last ten years, a new job category has been [1] ________________: professional fashion blogger. The story of one of the very first professional bloggers is an inspiration to young people everywhere who are [2] ________________ with how to make a good living while also doing something that is important to them.

In 2007, Imran Amed, a young Canadian-British citizen who had recently moved to London, decided to take advantage of some free time he had while he wasn't busy working at his job. He sat down in his living room and began to write about something he was passionately [3] ________________ in: fashion. Sitting on his sofa, he created a blog that allowed him to communicate with readers who shared his fascination with the fashion industry. Naturally, at the beginning, his readers were mainly his friends and family. But because of his ability to tell interesting and perceptive stories that made readers want to keep on reading, his blog was soon [4] ________________ by many people, and by professionals in the industry.

In time, advertisers began to pay Amed's blog, *The Business of Fashion*, for the opportunity to connect with all those readers and potential clients. Amed was also an excellent interviewer. His interviews with Karl Lagerfeld, Natalie Massenet, Nick Knight, and other giants in the fashion industry became another great attraction to his blog. Designers were willing to be [5] ________________ by him because his questions and comments were relevant, intelligent, and [6] ________________ by his passion for fashion.

Imran Amed, accepting the Business of Fashion Media Award at the 2016 CFDA Fashion Awards

Today, professionals in 200 countries consider *The Business of Fashion* to be required reading in order to keep up with the latest developments in fashion. Thirty employees now fill the demand for information on fashion. More recent fashion blogs like Chiara Ferragni's *The Blonde Salad* in Italy and Sabina Hernandez's blog *Te lo dije nena (I told you, girl)* in Argentina are now also very successful.

Potential professional bloggers, take note: passionate interest is fundamental to success. If you can discover your passion, then the power of that energy will be the magnet that captures and holds your readers' attention. That is exactly what happened one day when Imran Amed sat down and began to write a blog on his sofa.

B Read the article. Check (✓) the true statements according to the article. For the statements that are false, write the true information.

1. ☐ Imran Amed has always lived in London.

   ____

2. ☐ His family and friends are not interested in fashion and do not read about it.

   ____

3. ☐ Because Imran Amed knows how to tell an interesting story, many people began to read his blog.

   ____

4. ☐ Designers enjoy giving interviews to Imran Amed because his questions are intelligent and show that he is interested in fashion.

   ____

5. ☐ Chiara Ferragni's and Sabina Hernandez's blogs were started before *The Business of Fashion*.

   ____

6. ☐ If you want to be a professional blogger, the most important thing you will need for success is money.

   ____

5 Join these sentences with *who* or *that*. Add a comma wherever one is needed.

broadcast presenter

junior newspaper reporter

Examples:

Broadcast presenters are journalists.

They report the news on television.

Broadcast presenters are journalists who report the news on television.

A junior newspaper reporter should be curious.

He or she is often new to journalism.

A junior newspaper reporter, who is often new to journalism, should be curious.

1. An editorial director chooses only the most interesting stories.

   He or she tells the reporters what news stories to cover.

   ____

   ____

2. A game animator is a skilled artist.

   He or she creates detailed graphics for computer games.

   ____

   ____

3. A storyboard artist is a creative person.

   He or she illustrates plans for individual scenes for a movie.

   ____

   ____

4. Stunt people perform dangerous moves in films and TV shows.

   The films and shows have a lot of action scenes.

   ____

   ____

5. TV sitcoms include actors and actresses.

   They are recognized by television viewers around the world.

   ____

   ____

6 Match the definitions with the jobs.

1. a cinematographer __g__
2. a film editor _____
3. a gossip columnist _____
4. a graphic designer _____
5. a club DJ _____
6. a band manager _____
7. a web content manager _____
8. a talk show host _____

a. a journalist who specializes in reporting on the personal lives of famous people
b. someone who plays music in a dance club
c. someone that helps a movie director put together the best "takes"
d. a person who is in charge of choosing the text and pictures on a website
e. a TV personality who invites guests to come on his or her program
f. a person who takes care of business for a band
g. a person who operates the main camera during shooting
h. someone that creates the design for a printed work

7 Choose a job from Exercise 6 or another job you're interested in. In the first paragraph, describe the job. In the second paragraph, explain why the job interests you. Use relative clauses in some of your descriptions.

I'd like to be a band manager for a rock or pop band. Band managers are the people who schedule concerts and shows for bands. They also help bands make creative decisions about things like CD covers, magazine interviews, and even music. In addition, band managers who know people in the music business can help a band become successful.

This job interests me because I love music, and I enjoy being around people who sing and play instruments. Also, I'm organized and reliable, and I think that I have the skills that a good band manager needs.

8 Describe six steps in the process of renovating a restaurant. Use the passive form of the verbs given below.

1. First, a renovation plan is approved. (a renovation plan / approve)
2. Next, ______________________________ (new walls / build)
3. Then ______________________________ (the walls / paint)
4. After that, ______________________________ (new lighting / install)
5. Then ______________________________ (new furniture / deliver)
6. Finally, ______________________________ (the restaurant / reopen)

15 A law must be passed!

1 What should be done about each situation? Write sentences about these pictures, giving your opinion. Use the passive form with *should, shouldn't,* or *ought to.*

1 Leaving large items on the sidewalk

2 Eating on the subway

3 Playing loud music in your apartment

4 Letting dogs run without leashes

1. *People shouldn't be allowed to leave large items on the sidewalk.* OR
People ought to be required to take large items to designated dumps.
2. ______________________________
3. ______________________________
4. ______________________________

2 Make recommendations about the situations in these pictures. Use the passive form with *has to, has got to, must,* or *mustn't.*

1

2

3

4

1. A law has to be passed to prevent people from losing their homes. OR
Something must be done to repair abandoned homes.

2. ______________________________

3. ______________________________

4. ______________________________

3 Think of four things that you have strong opinions about. Write your opinions and explain your reasons for them. Use passive modals.

Example: *In my opinion, cell phones shouldn't be allowed in class.*
They distract students from the lesson.

1. I feel that ______________________________
____
2. I think that ______________________________
____
3. In my opinion, ______________________________
____
4. I don't think that ______________________________
____

4 Respond to these opinions by giving a different one of your own. Use expressions from the box.

That's interesting, but I think . . .
That's not a bad idea. On the other hand, I feel . . .
You may have a point. However, I think . . .
Do you? I'm not sure . . .

1. **A:** Everyone should be required to study Chinese.
   B: *You may have a point. However, I think that English is more useful for traveling.*
2. **A:** People mustn't be allowed to write unkind things about others on social networking sites.
   B: ______________________________
3. **A:** Public transportation should be provided free of charge.
   B: ______________________________
4. **A:** I think people ought to be required to buy hybrid cars.
   B: ______________________________
5. **A:** In my opinion, all plastic containers should be banned.
   B: ______________________________

5 Getting revenge

A Skim the web posts. What is a revenge story? Why is each of these stories a revenge story?

DO YOU HAVE A REVENGE STORY? SHARE IT!

1. Marcy: I used to have a friend who was a lot of fun. She always loved to go out to eat. There was just one small problem: Every time the server brought the check, she would say, "Uh-oh! I don't have enough money with me. Can I pay you back later?" This was OK the first and second time it happened, but these excuses happened again and again.

I finally got my revenge. The next time we went out for dinner, I said that I had forgotten my wallet. She was shocked, but she paid the check. However, she has never called me to go out again. I guess she was a moocher – a person who always tries to get someone else to pay.

2. Jonathan: My neighbors used to keep rabbits in their yard, but they treated them very badly. Rabbit pens should be cleaned regularly, but these rabbits were dirty, and the smell was really terrible. Worse, I noticed that the rabbits didn't have enough to eat or drink. When I complained to my neighbors, they said, "It's not your problem."

When I called the animal protection society, they said they would investigate. I waited a week, but nothing happened. One night, I stole the rabbits and took them home. The next day I gave them to a local pet store.

3. Chad: I was having problems sleeping because of a dripping noise coming from my air conditioner. I thought the air conditioner needed to be repaired, so I called a technician. She couldn't find anything wrong with it, but she said the dripping was coming from the apartment above me. I asked my neighbor to have his air conditioner checked, but he said, "If you can't sleep, that's your problem!"

The following day I climbed a ladder and turned off the electricity inside the air conditioner. My neighbor had to call the technician to turn it on, and when she did, she also fixed the dripping. It cost him a few dollars, but it was worth it!

B Read the comments. Do you agree or disagree? Write *A* (agree) or *D* (disagree).

_____ **1.** Marcy shouldn't have pretended to lose her wallet. She should have spoken with her friend and told her it was time she paid for a meal.

_____ **2.** I think Marcy did exactly what she ought to have done. Moochers must be taught a lesson!

_____ **3.** People mustn't be permitted to steal. Jonathan made a big mistake, didn't he?

_____ **4.** If people don't take care of their animals, something has got to be done. However, I don't think he should have stolen the rabbits.

_____ **5.** Sometimes neighbors must be taught a lesson. Chad didn't hurt anybody, so I think his nasty neighbor got what he deserved.

_____ **6.** You may have a point about some neighbors, but I think Chad should have called the manager of his building.

C Do you think getting revenge – doing something mean to someone in return – is acceptable behavior? Why or why not?

____

____

____

6 Add tag questions to these statements.

1. Bullying is a serious problem, ___isn't it___?
2. The city doesn't provide enough services for elderly people, ___does it___?
3. You can easily spend all your money on food and rent, ________________?
4. Some unemployed people don't really want to work, ________________?
5. Health care is getting more and more expensive, ________________?
6. There are a lot of homeless people downtown, ________________?
7. Some schools have overcrowded classrooms, ________________?
8. Laws should be passed to reduce street crime, ________________?

7 Nouns and verbs

A Complete the chart.

Noun	Verb	Noun	Verb
advertisement	advertise	________	pollute
________	bully	prohibition	________
________	improve	provision	________
offense	________	________	require
permission	________	________	vandalize

B Write sentences with tag questions using words from the chart. Use four of the nouns and four of the verbs.

1. Bicyclists should be required to wear helmets, shouldn't they?
2. ________________________________
3. ________________________________
4. ________________________________
5. ________________________________
6. ________________________________
7. ________________________________
8. ________________________________
9. ________________________________

8 Give one reason for and one reason against these opinions.

1. Children should be made to study a foreign language in primary school.
   For: *It would help children understand other cultures.*
   Against: *I don't think it would be easy to find enough teachers.*
2. Schools should punish students who bully other children.
   For: ______________________
   Against: ______________________
3. More tax money ought to be spent on cleaning up vandalism.
   For: ______________________
   Against: ______________________
4. Stray animals should be cared for in animal shelters.
   For: ______________________
   Against: ______________________

9 Complete the conversation. Use passive modals and tag questions.

Gina: You know, I just moved into this new apartment building, and I thought everything would be really great now.

Alec: What's the problem?

Gina: Well, yesterday, the manager gave me a copy of the house rules. I found out that I can't park my moped on the sidewalk in front of the building anymore.

Alec: But people shouldn't ______________________ (permit) to park their bikes or mopeds there.

Gina: Why not? There isn't any other place to park, ______________________? I guess I'll have to park on the street now.

Alec: I'm sorry that parking somewhere else will be inconvenient, but don't you agree that people shouldn't ______________________ (allow) to block the sidewalk or the entrance to the building?

Gina: Well, you may have a point, but parking spaces for all types of cycles need ______________________ (provide) for renters here. All renters with a car have a parking space, ______________________?

Alec: Well, yes, you're right. You should go to the next renters' meeting and discuss the issue with everyone else.

Gina: That's not a bad idea. My voice ought ______________________ (hear) as much as anyone else's – I think I will!

16 Reaching your goals

1 Match each profession with the correct achievement.

☐ actor	☐ student	☐ volunteer
☐ parent	☐ nurse	☑ high school counselor

1. I've managed to help hundreds of students get into college. _high school counselor_
2. I was able to clean litter from dozens of beaches over the last three years. ____________
3. I managed to maintain an A average during my last four years of school. ____________
4. I've been able to work with many of my favorite movie stars. ____________
5. I've managed to teach my children how to be responsible citizens. ____________
6. I've been able to help sick people feel better. ____________

2 Choosing a job

A Complete the chart with your own ideas.

Job	Goals of people with this profession	
1. social worker	_help people_	____________
2. university professor	_educate people_	____________
3. small-business owner	____________	____________
4. emergency-room nurse	____________	____________

B Complete these sentences with your ideas from part A. Try to add more details.

1. As a social worker, Jane hopes she'll _have helped poor and elderly people in her community._
   She'd also like to have ____________
2. As a university professor three years from now, Paul hopes he'll have ____________
   ____
   He'd also like to have ____________
   ____
3. By this time next year, Jake, a small business owner, would like to have ____________
   ____
   In addition, he hopes he'll have ____________
   ____
4. In the next five years, Amy, an emergency-room nurse, hopes she'll have ____________
   ____
   In addition, she'd like to have ____________

3 Write two paragraphs about an issue that is important to you. In the first paragraph, describe a past achievement related to that issue. In the second paragraph, describe a goal.

Last year, I began volunteering at a local animal shelter. I managed to help find homes for over twenty cats and dogs in one year. It was an incredibly rewarding experience.

In the next few years, I hope to help more animals find homes. I'd like to have placed a hundred pets in homes over the next four years.

4 The challenge of a lifetime

A Scan the first paragraph of the article. Where is Rupert Isaacson from? Where are his parents from? Where did he go?

RUPERT ISAACSON

Rupert Isaacson is a man who has faced a major challenge in his life. The son of parents who were born in Africa, he grew up in London and in the English countryside, where he discovered his love of horses. Because he grew up hearing so many fascinating memories about Africa from his parents, he went there and lived with nomadic people called the Bushmen of the Kalahari Desert. He then wrote a book, *The Healing Land*, about his experiences with the Bushmen and the problems of survival they face in the twenty-first century.

By the year 2000, Rupert was already managing to make a living as a journalist, writing articles and guidebooks about Africa and India. It was in India that he met his wife, Kristin. Today, they live with their son, Rowan, just outside of Austin, Texas, in the U.S. But Rupert faced the greatest challenge of his life when, at the age of two, Rowan was diagnosed with autism, a condition that affects people's ability to communicate and interact socially with others.

Rupert discovered that spending time with horses and riding them was helping Rowan. The presence of the horses was very calming to the boy. Rupert also knew that the Bushmen of the Kalahari possessed great knowledge about healing. He thought that if he could find a group of people with healing powers and a great knowledge of horses, there could be a possibility of helping his son. Unfortunately, the Bushmen of the Kalahari do not have horses.

So the family set off for Mongolia, where horses have been important for thousands of years. Rupert has written about this journey dedicated to helping his son in *Horse Boy*, and he has produced a documentary of the same name. In the film, viewers have the opportunity to see the family traveling in Mongolia, riding horses, and meeting healers in order to help Rowan.

Because working with horses has helped Rowan, Rupert established The Horse Boy Foundation at his ranch in Texas. It is a school that teaches people how to use horses for healing. In addition to writing another book, *The Long Ride Home*, about traveling with Rowan to Africa, Australia, and Arizona in the U.S., Rupert has also produced the documentary *Endangerous*, with Rowan as host, about dangerous animals that are threatened with extinction. Rupert Isaacson has managed to discover the secret of turning one challenge into many accomplishments.

B Read the article. What is the challenge that Rupert Isaacson faced? What was one of the solutions to this challenge that Rupert found?

Challenge: ______________________________

Solution: ______________________________

C Answer the questions.

1. How does autism affect people?

____

2. Why did Rupert's family go to Mongolia?

____

3. What is the purpose of The Horse Boy Foundation?

____

4. What does Rowan do in *Endangerous*?

____

5. List three accomplishments of Rupert Isaacson.

____

5 Choose the correct word.

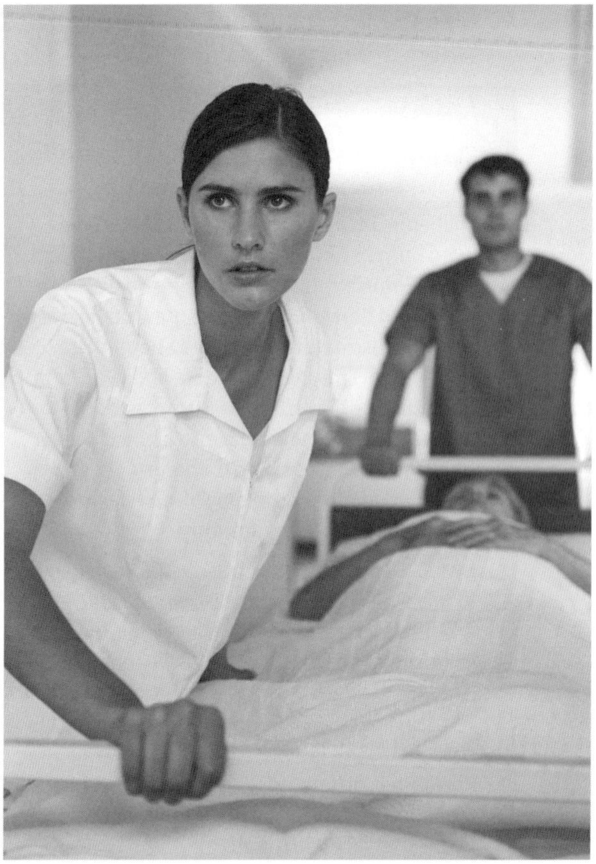

1. It's not good to be ______________________ if you're an emergency-room nurse. (courageous / timid / upbeat)
2. If teachers are going to be successful, they have to be ______________________. (dependent / rigid / resourceful)
3. You have to be ______________________ if you work as a volunteer. (adaptable / cynical / unimaginative)
4. If you take a job far from your family and friends, you have to be ______________________. (compassionate / dependent / self-sufficient)
5. One of the most important things about working with children is being positive and not ______________________. (adaptable / cynical / resourceful)
6. Being a role model for troubled youths requires someone who is strong and ______________________. (compassionate / insensitive / timid)

6 Read each sentence. Write *A* for achievement or *G* for goal.

1. I've been able to provide clean water to three villages during my time as a Peace Corps volunteer. _____
2. By the time I'm 35, I'd like to have lived in a culture that's very different from my own. _____
3. While I was working abroad in Tokyo, I managed to learn to speak Japanese fluently. _____
4. After my time with Habitat for Humanity, I hope to have made a significant and positive difference in people's lives. _____
5. I'd like to have gotten another degree in two years. _____
6. I hope I'll have gotten married by the time I'm 30. _____

7 Accomplishments and goals

A Match the verbs with the nouns. Write the collocations. (More than one answer may be possible.)

Verb	Noun	
buy	a change	**1.** buy a house
get	debts	**2.** ______
learn	a house	**3.** ______
make	a promotion	**4.** ______
meet	new skills	**5.** ______
pay off	someone special	**6.** ______

B Write one sentence about an accomplishment and another sentence about a goal. Use the words in part A and your own ideas.

1. My sister and her husband have managed to save enough money to buy a house. I expect to have bought a house within five years.
2. ______
3. ______
4. ______
5. ______
6. ______

8 Personal portraits

A Write three sentences about the accomplishments of someone you know very well. Use the present perfect or simple past.

By investing his money carefully, my neighbor Enrico was able to retire at 40. Since then, he has managed to set up an organization that helps find jobs for people who are homeless. In addition, he has volunteered his time at a homeless shelter in the city.

B Write three sentences about things the same person would like to have achieved in ten years. Use the future perfect or *would like to have* + past participle.

Enrico would like to have started an organization to provide scholarships for needy college students by the time he's 50. He hopes to travel a lot, too. In fact, he hopes he'll have traveled all through Southeast Asia.